THE
COLLECTED
POEMS
OF
ANNE
WILKINSON

THE
COLLECTED
POEMS
OF
ANNE
WILKINSON

THE
COLLECTED
POEMS
OF
Anne Wilkinson

AND
A
PROSE
MEMOIR

Edited, with an introduction,
by A. J. M. Smith

ST. MARTIN'S PRESS
1968
NEW YORK

FIRST PUBLISHED IN THE UNITED STATES OF AMERICA IN 1968

Library of Congress Catalogue Card No. 68–28797

Designed by William Toye

Printed in the United Kingdom

Contents

Contents

The Hangman Ties the Holly 1955

Contents

Poems from Periodicals and Anthologies

vii

Contents

Poems from the Notebooks

Contents

A Prose Memoir

Notes

ix

Preface

ANNE GIBBONS WILKINSON was born in Toronto in 1910. Her early childhood was spent in London, Ontario, and she received a somewhat informal and varied education in a number of English and American schools. She published two volumes of poetry, *Counterpoint to Sleep* in 1951 and *The Hangman Ties the Holly* in 1955. In addition to her verse she published *Lions in the Way* (1956), an informal history of the Osler family, with which she herself was connected, and *Swann and Daphne* (1960), a modern fairy tale for children. She died in 1961. 'Four Corners of My World', an autobiographical fragment she was working on at the time of her death, was published in *The Tamarack Review* and is included here along with her poems. It is a less formal but equally evocative expression of the gaiety, wit, and charm that made Anne Wilkinson so radiant a person.

With the addition of the uncollected poems to her two volumes of verse and the poems published in *The Tamarack Review* and *The Oxford Book of Canadian Verse*, the present volume brings together everything Anne Wilkinson wrote in verse with the exception of half a score of pieces she herself had recognized as inferior and as many more fragments and unfinished sketches.

I have examined three notebooks containing drafts of *The Hangman Ties the Holly* and have added a few poems that appeared in them but were not included in the book. Among these are such fine poems as 'March, April, June', 'Old Adam', the long continuation of 'Letter to My Children', and a few others.

Preface

There are also a number of interesting drafts, sketches, and work sheets, particularly of the ambitious and original poems 'Swimming Lesson', 'Lens', and, among the later unpublished pieces, 'When a Body Breaks'. I have followed the text, in every case, of the published volumes and the versions printed in periodicals or anthologies. The various typescripts (many with pencilled corrections) of the late unprinted poems leave little doubt as to which is the final and preferred text. In a few cases I have indicated variant readings in the notes.

It remains to thank Mr. John Gray for his encouragement and patience; Mr. Kildare Dobbs, the editor who saw the manuscript of *The Hangman Ties the Holly* through the press, for assistance in more ways than one; Mr. George Woodcock, editor of *Canadian Literature*, for permitting me to use (with some changes and additions) my essay 'A Reading of Anne Wilkinson', which appeared in the Autumn 1961 issue of *Canadian Literature*; and finally to the executors of the estate of Anne Wilkinson for lending me the MSS. and notebooks containing the poems now published for the first time.

Drummond Point,   A. J. M. SMITH
Lake Memphremagog, Quebec

Introduction

A READING OF ANNE WILKINSON

WHEN I HEARD OF the death of Anne Wilkinson I read once again, and at a single sitting, all the poems she had written – her first small collection *Counterpoint to Sleep* published in 1951, the volume of 1955 *The Hangman Ties the Holly*, her three lyric sequences in *The Tamarack Review* No. 5 and No. 18, and later the notebooks and manuscripts containing the poems which are here published for the first time, pieces written mostly in the last year of her life.

I read with a newly sharpened awareness – an awareness of small, immensely significant details of imagery, music, language, and emotion. There is a stanza of Emily Dickinson which describes the strange clarification brought about by death, and it kept running in my head as a sort of counterpoint to what I was reading:

> *We noticed smallest things,*
> *Things overlooked before,*
> *By this great light upon our minds*
> *Italicized, as 'twere.*

I could not help thinking how well these lines applied not only to my own state of mind but to one of the special qualities and peculiar virtues of Anne Wilkinson's poems – their being saturated, as it were, with light, a radiance of the mind, cast often on small, familiar things, or things overlooked before, and reflected back into the mind and heart.

'The poet's eye is crystal,' she noted in 'Lens', one of the few poems that state an explicit *æsthetique*, and her 'long duty' and 'daily chore' is to keep and cherish her good lens. The crystal eye, the craftsman's lens, the light that animates them, and the green world on which it falls: these are the instruments and materials, and the colours and lights that flash through her verse. She never knew the tragedy of not living in a sensual world. It is a sensuousness of the eye that most vividly brings her world to life, but the æther through which this light vibrates is a tremor of the mind and the vision of her green world is made fruitful by love.

In the first lines of the first poem in *The Hangman Ties the Holly* she announces one of the two main themes of her book:

> *Who has the cunning to apprehend*
> *Even everyday easy things*
> *Like air and wind and a fool*
> *Or the structure and colour of a simple soul?*

> *New laid lovers sometimes see,*
> *In a passion of light . . .*

Light is everywhere here a symbol of truth, reality, and, above all, life. *Green* signifies Nature, sensation, happiness, grace, and again life. If these aspects of her sensibility make one think of Vaughan or Traherne in the one case and of Andrew Marvell in the other, the newness, freshness, and uniqueness of her vision are not diminished but enhanced.

A traditional background is a help, not a hindrance, when it is entered into with all one's wits about one and purified by the senses. Earth, air, fire, and water have an immediate sensational significance in the poetry of Anne Wilkinson – as well as a medieval and metaphysical one. In a poem that develops out of an aphorism by Empedocles – *I was born a boy, and a maiden, a plant and a bird, and a darting fish in the sea* – she enters, through the twin gates of sensation and wit, into the phenomenal world and becomes a part of its life:

> *Yet always I huff out the flame with breath*
> *   as live*
> *And green as Irish grass, recalling the gills*
> *Of my youth when I was a miner*
> *Deep in the hills of the sea.*

The union of the four elements and her own identification with them is everywhere assumed, but occasionally it is explicitly, concretely, and dynamically *stated*, as in the *fiat* of the last stanza of 'Poem in Three Parts':

> *The stone in my hand*
> *IS my hand*
> *And stamped with tracings of*
> *A once greenblooded frond,*
> *Is here, is gone, will come,*
> *Was fire, and green, and water,*
> *Will be wind.*

This is as close perhaps as this poet has come to a religious statement – or at least to a religious statement untouched by irony – but hers is the classic religion of Empedocles, Heraclitus, and Lucretius. What it celebrates is a metamorphosis. Over and over again she descends into the earth like Flora or Eurydice or merges white flesh, red blood, into the leafy green of a tree like Daphne:

> *Let the world go limp, put it to rest,*
> *Give it a soft wet day and while it sleeps*
> *Touch a drenched leaf; . . .*

> *Before you turn*
> *Uncurl prehensile fingers from the tree,*
> *Cut your name on bark, search*
> *The letters for your lost identity.*

The twenty or so stanzas which form the 'postscript' to *Letter to My Children* and which, regrettably, I think, were dropped from the *Hangman* volume, afford many other illustrations of this sensuous imagery. The greatest gift she can bequeath her children is:

> *Five full and fathomed senses,*
> *Precision instruments*
> *To chart the wayward course*
> *Through rock and moss and riddles . . .*

Introduction

There is a flowing together and intermingling of the senses in some of her most characteristic expressions as, for example, in the magical stanza beginning:

> *You'll shiver but you'll hear*
> *The sharp white nails of the moon*
> *Scratch the slate of midnight water . . .*

or in the image of the eye, the hungry eye, as tiger:

> *Uncage the tiger in your eye*
> *And tawny, night and day,*
> *Stalk the landscape for the contour*
> *Of a fern or arm . . .*

The poem is long and somewhat discursive, perhaps, but it both epitomizes and illustrates the poet's sensibility and wit and has its own delightful ingenuity. Images derived from an urban sophistication are used for the expression of a universal and quite classical hedonism. Praise of the senses as the source of joy and wisdom is recorded in many of the poems – usually in the language of romantic convention. 'The ear . . . will mark the drop in pitch of towns adrift in fog.' The 'luminous dial' of the eye will read the 'gold numerals of dawn Thin on the face of the midnight watch', and nose must:

> *Smell the vigour*
> *Packed in snow at noon and metal*
> *In the air*
> *When stars show up for duty*
> *On the dim lit wards of winter . . .*

For Anne Wilkinson the body and its senses were the instruments through which nature and reality entered the mind and became a part of being. 'I put on my body and go forth To seek my blood,' she writes in the lovely poem *The Red and the Green*:

> *I walk the hollow subway*
> *Of the ear . . .*

xvi

Skin is minstrel, sings
Tall tales and shady
Of the kings of Nemi Wood. . . .

My new green arteries

Fly streamers from the maypole of my arms,
From head to toe
My blood sings green . . .

My blood sings green: this is one aspect of her poetry – its intimate sensuous identification with life as a growth out of the earth; and it implies a Pan-ic or Lawrencian forgetfulness of the non-living, dry, and essentially irrelevant intellection of much of our routine living. But knowledge, intellect, and the motions of thought are by no means absent from this poetry. They are seen of course in the buried literary allusions and the puns. The former are perhaps not essential, but they are not merely orna-mental or snobbish either – they italicize and connect rather than make an initial or final assertion – and it is good to find con-firmation of one's feelings in Sir James Frazer, Mother Goose, Shakespeare, and the author of 'Greensleeves'. The puns, as elsewhere in these poems,* not only give an impression of liveli-ness, sharpness, and wit, but convey with greater precision and intensity, and immensely greater compactness, a relationship that might take clauses and sentences instead of a single word to get across. *The curd and why of memory*, for instance, presents the mental gropings after something forgotten with an almost physio-logical suggestion of the tremblings of the membrane of nerves and brain.

This poetry of green thoughts in a green shade is connected also with the red of the earth and of blood. The identification of the poet with nature is sensuous and emotional. It is achieved in love, and it is achieved in death. These two themes – and a union of them both in a sort of love-hate relationship with death

---

* Some examples: 'new laid lover', 43; 'the warm gulf seam of love', 54; 'happily lived ever waterward', 55; 'the curd and why of memory', 68 – to cite only a few.

– are found in some of the earliest of the poems as well as in some truly terror-inspiring poems which give a sombre intensity to *The Hangman Ties the Holly*. They are found too, as might have been expected, in the last, uncollected, poems.

LOVE, IN THE POETRY of Anne Wilkinson, is sometimes, as in 'Strangers', a game of wit, but it is always also a sensuous involvement, not a twining of bodies and minds only but a mingling with the green sap of Nature in a wholly holy communion. This is the significance of the delightful and lovely poem beginning 'In June and gentle oven . . .'.

> *In June and gentle oven*
> *Summer kingdoms simmer*
> *As they come*
> *And flower and leaf and love*
> *Release*
> *Their sweetest juice . . .*

The music is impeccable. Presently there is one faintly sinister image, which soon we realize is intended to hint at the necessary serpent in every Eden, –

> *An adder of a stream*
> *Parts the daisies . . .*

But lovers are protected by Nature, instinct, and joy, and are 'saved':

> *And where, in curve of meadow,*
> *Lovers, touching, lie,*
> *A church of grass stands up*
> *And walls them, holy, in.*

The closing stanza of this poem is one of the most beautiful expressions in modern poetry of the divinity of love achieved in the sensuous community of the green world:

> *Then two in one the lovers lie*
> *And peel the skin of summer*

With their teeth
And suck its marrow from a kiss
So charged with grace
The tongue, all knowing
Holds the sap of June
Aloof from seasons, flowing.

Something of this fertile richness is found in a later love poem
– the sequence of five lyrics entitled 'Variations on a Theme'.
Here, however, the pure and innocent religion of love and nature
has been clouded by an intense awareness, amounting almost to a
foreknowledge, of death, and there is an air of faint desperation
in the spells and magic rituals that are tried as exorcisms.

The poem is a series of variations on a sentence of Thoreau:
'A man needs only to be turned around once with his eyes shut
to be lost in this world.' The key words are *turned* and *lost*. Each
of the five lyrics explores one of the ways of being lost. Thoreau
thought of losing the world in the Christian sense of a spiritual
achievement, but there are many ways of being lost – some are a
kind of ecstasy and all are bewildering. In the first of the variations
it is childhood's 'first flinging of the blood about in circles', a
recollection of games in the green meadow when the child spins
round and round in dizzying circles until the world and his own
identity are lost. The second and fourth lyrics are visions of horror
– the second of death, the fourth of madness.

From arteries in graves, columns
Rose to soil the sky; and down
Their fluted sides the overflow
Slid to earth, unrolled and spread
On stalk and stone its plushy red.

The elegance of the writing enhances the horror of this second
section, but the intensity increases still more in the nightmare-
like fourth:

. . . where above me one black crow
Had cawed my spring, two dirty doves
Sang daintily. I stoned the birds

Introduction

> But no stone hit, for of white gloves
> My hands were made; I stole a stick
> To break the sky; it did not crack;
> I could not curse — though I was lost,
> Had trespassed on some stranger's dream . . .

The third section, like the first, is a happy one. It deals with the magical transformation of being 'lost' in love. Significantly, it is the only poem in the sequence in which the protagonist is *we* not *I*. It is a very beautiful poem, and short enough to quote in full:

> We shut our eyes and turned once round
> And were up borne by our down fall.
> Such life was in us on the ground
> That while we moved, earth ceased to roll,
> And oceans lagged, and all the flames
> Except our fire, and we were lost
> In province that no settler names.

The fifth poem rises almost directly out of this one and develops the theme of death more simply and traditionally than it had been treated in the second and fourth:

> Death turned me first, will twirl me last
> And throw me down beneath the grass
> And strip me of this stuff, this dress
> I am, although its form be lost.

IF THE GREEN, light-riddled poetry in which Anne Wilkinson celebrated life and the love of life makes one think of Marvell and Vaughan, she is also, like Webster (and not in her last poems only), much possessed by death. I mentioned earlier the love-hate relationship with death that seems almost inherent in her sensibility and that animates in a truly terror-inspiring way a few of her most powerful poems, 'The Pressure of Night', 'Strangers', 'Topsoil to the Wind', as well as the recent deceptively light and witty 'Notes on Robert Burton's *The Anatomy of Melancholy*' and

xx

the brilliant 'A Cautionary Tale'. To these we must now add some of the poems written in her last year when she knew her illness mortal – 'Summer Storm', with its terrible evocation of pain pressing 'on nerve ends in the brain' –

> *Skull's skin is paper thin*
> *Migraine is seeping in –*

and 'Waking', 'A Room for Sleep', and the fearful poem beginning 'Accustom the grey coils Locked in the skull To the silence' and ending

> *the swelling*
> *Predicts at its pressing point*
> *Hoarded night bursting, the*
> *black sky unloading*
> *Its stars till the skull is alight.*

The sequence 'A Sorrow of Stones', and particularly its culminating poem 'When a Body Breaks', represent the most original and terrible of the later poems:

> *It is other than I had imagined. I thought*
> *To travel behind two plumed white horses,*
> *I thought to lie like cream in a long black hearse*
> *I had not calculated on this*
> *Fall without end.*

Yet even in these final poems Anne Wilkinson was able to integrate the witness of all the senses into an affirming testimony of the beauty and richness of life. They consolidate her position among the small group of women poets who have written of love and death with a peculiarly feminine intuition, an accuracy, and an elegance that do not hide but enhance the intensity of the emotion – Emily Dickinson, Christina Rossetti, Elinor Wylie, and Leonie Adams. Her work as a whole puts her, certainly, in the forefront of contemporary Canadian poets. She has helped us to be a little more aware and hence a little more civilized. Her poems are a legacy whose value can never be diminished.

COUNTERPOINT

TO

SLEEP

1951

Summer acres

like

I

These acres breathe my family,
Holiday with seventy summers' history.
My blood lives here,
Sunned and veined three generations red
Before my bones were formed.

My eyes are wired to the willow
That wept for my father,
My heart is boughed by the cedar
That covers with green limbs the bones of my children,
My hands are white with a daisy, sired
By the self same flower my grandfather loved;

My ears are tied to the tattle of water
That echoes the vows of ancestral lovers,
My skin is washed by a lather of waves
That bathed the blond bodies of uncles and aunts
And curled on the long flaxen hair of my mother;

My feet step soft on descendants of grass
That was barely brushed
By the wary boots of a hummingbird woman,
The Great Great Grandmother
Of my mid-century children.

II

September born, reared in the sunset hour,
I was the child of old men heavy with honour;
I mourned the half mast time of their death and sorrowed
A season for leaves, shaking their scarlet flags
From green virility of trees.

As ears spring cartilaged from skulls
So my ears spring from the sound of water
And the whine of autumn in the family tree.
How tired, how tall grow the trees
Where the trees and the family are temples
Whose columns will tumble, leaf over root to their ruin.

Here, in my body's home my heart dyes red
The last hard maple in their acres.
Where birch and elm and willow turn,
Gently bred, to gold against the conifers,
I hail my fathers, sing their blood to the leaf.

Winter sketch

ROCKCLIFFE, OTTAWA

Down domestic roads the snow plough, snorting
Stacks a crop of winter, spills it high
To hedgerows alped with lilies; in the valley
White is wag, is daisy till
The sun aloft and hot with husbandry
Beheads the flowers.

Behind the plough the cold air flies a spume
As soft and adamant as swans
Where snow's vocation is to etherize
The wood and choke the town's
Hard arteries with drifts of chloroform.
And all the long excessive day the ploughman
Steers his dreaming over the hill
To the faraway hour that carries his frostbite home.

Such storm of white
Bound by the black extravagance of night
Makes winding sheet our myth-told-many-a-bed-time tale
Till April babble swells the shroud to breast
So milky full the whole north swills, licking
A world of sugar from encrusted nipples
Springful and swollen with love.

And tusked with icicles, the houses here
Bog stuporous in slow white sand, guard

Their docile lawns with walls that boast
Immaculate conception in a cloud
Made big by polar ghost.
In suburb of the forest, men walk shy,
Dismembered by two worlds;
Only the uncurled ears of children hear
The coyotes mating in a neighbour's acre,
Theirs the only hands whose thumbs work free
To sculpt a tower leaning tipsy with unPisan laughter;
And being young, flexible pink tongues
Rename a carrot, nose;
Nose on hump of snow they crystal christen
Christ, the stillborn man;
Then herd their feet to kick the undefiled
When eyes still whey with vision see
That chastity, though white, is wormed with sleep.

O watch the child lie down and lusty swing
His arms to angel in his image, sing
'I dare the snow my wings to keep.'

A *folk tale*

WITH A WARNING TO LOVERS

.

I wish to tell
In words of one syllable
The plight of two lovers,
But like a war of roses
Love is never
At this or any
Season, a simple tale.

Yet these were lovers
Scaled to commonplace dimensions, wrecked
On nothing stranger than a reef
Of love's unreason;
And they were wide aware
Of scarlet, brighter on the heart
When fusion follows the homing swing of flesh
From cerebral skies apart;
They'd watched the waning moon's
Face fade from the earth and the earth
Still pale from the moon, embrace the dark.

O they determined on a bliss
Above the common sweetness of two mouths
And all the dear etceteras of a kiss.
But why their greed was greater, why
They ventured farther

Than the garden love allows
I don't pretend to know,

I only know the tide of their desire
Swung miles beyond
The ebb and flow that love demands;
Each one a rocket in a space
Too rare to nourish roots or green
The tree of grace.
They seemed to think the farther off they ran
The greater the combustion
When they doubled back and crashed, mad
For Adam and Evening and the apple, red
And waiting for the hollow of a hand.

One lack a day alas,
The muscle of the heart cried 'Hold! Enough!'
And though the lovers turned
They did not move to take an outward step
But stood there, stiff and still
And gazing, each at Eden on a different hill.

It was a sullen Monday afternoon
It happened. Say a quarrel
Enacted in the teeth of an ill wind
Caught them cold – and spine to spine.

8

In half the time it takes to sneeze
Their backs were joined, locked, laced, inseparable.

They were not One,
All warm as lovers are at dawn
But One as are sad Siamese,
Irreparably linked twins.
No going away now knowing winters
March to April of surrender,
An end to turning
When the milky way to eyes is blocked
By pools of pupils, slippery with lies.

And in the streets and fields and on the beaches,
Like orators they fought
The polar pull of blood, the needle
Pointing North to recognition,
Twisting and yearning to trick the pulse
To the South position of love.
They bruised the beaches of their hearts
With breakers from endemic,
UnPacific storms, they slept,
Their torn roots bleeding, under eiderdowns
Theatrical with snow.
And each one dreamed at night the other cried
'O foe is me.'

9

But morning watched them waken
Closer cleaved than lovers lie, close
Enough to pick the years away with scraping,
Each at the other's scabless, yelping scar

Until one wholly Sunday afternoon
A second wind
Filled and lifted their lungs
In gusts that blew the bricks off chimney pots,
A supersonic rage above the wails
Of babes, new born;
Their voices violated doors, clouding
The weather in the street
That runs from their house of storm.

They called the law and doctors and quacks, pled
For a severing of joined, ill-mated backs.
But the wise men shook their heads,
'Whichever road you choose,' the sage fools said,
'The law, the knife, or a pack of cards
Stacked high to heaven with hearts –
There is a hitch –
To set one free, we're bound to cut
The other's cord to life.'
And all the jesters in the weeping town
Were dumb to tell them which.

When last I'd news of them
One lover looked to morning, one looked west.
When one lay down to sleep, the other fell.
For all I know they lie there yet,
On the home sweet hearth of hell.

Poem of anxiety

All morning I go walking in the jungle,
Loving and sweet with snakes, a wag
With winged malarial hosts,
With each insidious and daylight trap
I'm gay to tangle.

My whole and body being sings
In dapple of day jungle, laughs
To meet a death, unviolent, say
From an adder or a fretted insect's sting.

In acres spoked with noon
I ride the rim of danger, hoard
The pearl and swine of sweat
For one bright foe,
The striped, discerning tiger.

Though he stretches with the shadows
All the aftermath of the hay-high morning,
Yawning yet, nor turns
His golden menace from its lair,
The octave of his pads plays huge and soft
On my mouse timorous ear.

When night's at large in the jungle
I go fearful

Lest I kiss or claw his eye.
Too whoo, too whit, who's who
When all the jungle reeks?

Exposed by five white columns of the moon
Our tracks bear witness, prove
The mating of our spoor.
Clear as criss-cross lies our love
On the forest floor.

The up and down of it

As I came down
I met a man
Going up a narrow stair.
He wore a beard and hairy
Had the gall
To swear his name was God.
'Well met,' I answered, modest,
Lowering my catholic
Appetite of eyes,
'Alone, without a witness
I'll confess: I'm Mrs. Bloom,
The loitering Moon Goddess.'
He blushed, beard, gall and all
A heavenly red
And squeezed against the wall, afraid,
And I a simple witch
With only the silky power
To stroke the bat
That flaps the shutters in his belfry.
I mumboed a humble spell
I'd learned on earth from men
On burning terms with hell
Then let God pass.
Ascending on the right
He reached his tower.
I, two steps at a time,
Jumped my way to grass.

A *poet's-eye view*

You are earth, loam, actual fields
And we the green reed growing from your body;
You are solid, we are porous, ringed with chatter,
Stalks that echo water
Running in your under-worldly springs;
Your ribs crack in the sun, ridge with rain,
We lie boneless when our tissues fade;
You are stiff against the wind, we
Bend, arc'd with ague, by the storm
Are properly bowed down a day
Then up a daisy, green stalk straight, unbroken;
You, the earth, are bound to earth's own axis,
We, who grow our down roots deep in you
Are multi-headed, spray out seed like dandipuff
To tickle the fabulous thin highborn skin of air
Before we fall, point every potent feather
Back into its spawning bed, your tethered body;
You are warped with rock, the woof of you
Is ore; in soul's rough weather
Rock splits open at the giant tremor of the soil;
We, the green ones, laugh and add an inch
For each storm's death, our knowing nonsense blowing
On and off the lode of your mortality.

Still life

I'd love this body more
If graved in rigid wood
It could not move;
I'd cut it fresh in pine;
The little knots
Would show where muscles grew,
The hollows shadow ovals
Into eyes,
The grain be quick to point
The vein, be tendon's clue;
I'd whittle hair
A solid armoured hood
And nothing here profane,
Nor rend the wood
But bind my fluid form
To forest tree,
Be still and let its green blood
Enter me.

Orchids

I watch and mark the orchid; I have lamped
It carefully as a graded egg and stamped
The petal painted mauve as sick, not ill;
It vomits love-life from a dollar bill;

And for the White, red-centred White, red light
Is closer to the white of purity
Than this unhaloed flower. It boasts of snow
Although its tongue has licked the blood of swans.

The third, exclusive bronze, the fourth, a lake,
Wet, green with thunder, date since God last met
A tiger in the Plaza, lost His faith,
To paint with elegance the orchid for Arts sake.

Absolve the orchid butterfly! Blue, swift
And delicate! Ignore, forget the tuft
Of yellow fungus growing on the tree –
The wing in flight transcends the seed's morbidity!

Black and white

On still black water, water lilies
Are less lily than the swan;
Here, in still black water, two
White horses drinking, three white swans.

Two white horses turn and shake
The foaming from their mouths, three
Swans lift and spread snow-weighted wings,
Raise their breasts to drift on air,

Aloft, but lazy till the thud-
ding stallions' hoofs sound bass on the hill;
Earth echoes their pleasure, waked from languor;
Wind is waiting for

Assault of white birds' wings. Here
On still black sky, three white swans
Above two horses galloping.
One swan breaks the air with smothered

Strength of feathers, and they're off!
Look! Suddenly the stallions rise!
The chase is on! Two white horses,
Three swans flying on a still black sky.

Theme and variation

This is the noisy silence of a tree
The rustle in the fern is the noise of fear
A twig is a nerve; it snaps the heart to pounding.

This is the swollen silence under the sea;
The hush and push of pressure soundless, sounding,
Drowning the human splash, the man-made tear.

This is the spiral'd silence in a cave
Where silence echoes itself; it echoes a jest
As a shell forever uncoils the thread of a wave.

This is the silence of love, and though the ear part
It cannot hear, it will not hear the rest,
The pause between compulsions of the heart.

Lake song

Willow weep, let the lake lap up your green trickled tears.
Water, love, lip the hot roots, cradle the leaf;
Turn a new moon on your tongue, water, lick the deaf rocks,
With silk of your pebble-pitched song, water, wimple the beach;
Water, wash over the feet of the summer-bowed trees,
Wash age from the face of the stone.

I am a hearer of water;
My ears hold the sound and the feel of the sound of it mortally.
My skin is in love with lake water,
My skin is in love and it sings in the arms of its lover,
My skin is the leaf of the willow,
My nerves are the roots of the weeping willow tree.

My blood is a clot in the stone,
The blood of my heart is fused to a pit in the rock;
The lips of my lover can wear away stone,
My lover can free the blocked heart;
The leaf and the root and the red sap will run with lake water,
The arms of my lover will carry me home to the sea.

I *know not what to do, love*

I know not what to do, love
I know not what to do.
O hang your clothes on the hickory tree
And bathe in the shallow dew
And open an ear to the earth, love
That's beating under you.

I know not where to sleep, love
I know not where to sleep.
O cradle into the hay, love
And curl in close to the sheep
And the sheep and the little black lamb, love
Will bleat you into sleep.

I know not if I be, love
I know not if I be;
I do not know if I touch, love
Or if aught touches me.
O hang yourself on the weeping birch
And very soon you'll see.

La belle dame sans dormi

She did not dress
Except to wear
A word across her groin
She wore no jewels
But the snake
Living on her arm
She could not sleep
For sleep would watch
The flies stroll on her face
She did not dare
To lose her web
In that dark webbèd place.

Tower lullaby

Climb, as a child easy with circles
Spins to the tower
Or turn, an old man
Shaking out a route
With eighty journeys dragging at your back.

Swing to the tower
High as a child swings, higher and higher,
Swing on plenty of rope,
Or warily
Test the ascent
On the thread of your pulse.

Wheel, as a child is a swallow
Flying to spiral
Or plodding, string a necklace out of sweat
And stagger step by bead
Bead by step.

The stair is soft;
Little moon-lit lawns
Of lichen moss;
The stair is bare-faced stone;
So creak on curv-
ing rock or leap
From turf to the top, to the turret.

23

Then, panting, lean
The moment, prop
It on the parapet
Before it tumbles
Over and old again
Climb again
Young again
Sleep.

After reading Kafka

Here at my door I swing between obsessions:
Hall by day, corridor by night.
I am obsessed with exits, bound
To qualify the latitude of light,
To mourn the quantity of shadow
Beaked and flocked in flight across the meadow,

Spreading eagles on the stubble in the hall.
The hall is my terrain. I pace
Its length from where I am to who I'll be
When the sun falls from the sill;
It falls away from the window,
Window wedged in the narrowing ends of the wall;

I walk it every day, love summer months
When air and time and I are white with searching;
I name its flora, feed its fawn,
My eye is on the storm across the ceiling;
Leaking drains spread a cloud, streaks
Of hail crack and flake the paint in drifts
About the floor. I stare

Until an ounce of light and two of space
Trace a stain to the bearded face of God.
Pity him, a King, dependent now
On my erratic eye to right his halo;

He begs my eye to stay,
Begs my tongue call holy holy holy;
I yawn and as I turn he fades away.

The down-rays focus on the baseboard, spot
The dirt, the crunched and crunching cockroach, in
And on the wood in warts.
Though I remember in my head
This house where I was born, my feet forget
And pound the alleys, bruise their soles in byways
Leading nowhere from the hallowed hallway
And eyes forget their little blink of time,
The wasting of the worn thin planes of day
Flying lower, closer to the ground.

And yet, in June when time is light and big
I've come so near the end of it, if I'd a stick
I could have held the blind;
Before my last lid fell
I saw beyond the heel of Caliban to Ariel.

Light is my Love! I dallied, lost
The white years in a wink.
Do flora, deer and fawn breathe on?
Can they outwit the dark?

I shield a traitor
Am betrayed by the off-beat of a tock-sick heart.

Reassemble, join the scattered stems,
Fumble for an ankle in the black,
Put back the flesh; send broken feelers
Out to spy along the wall – Signal
If you touch an opening in the line to home!

Delicate as ears, fingers fest
(Walls are seeping)
Weeping blisters cry out from their tips,
Cry up up up the arm to the sky in my head;
I scold but still the blisters rise,
Hang glutinous in streamers from my eyes.

Can the wounded walk the voyage back?
Feel their door distinct from a hundred doors?
A key is cut for cunning
Is not strength to try a hundred locks.

(Did Noah save obsessions, two by two
Or did the green sea suck
At hall and corridor, deposit coral
Where the drowning drift from hide to seek?)

27

I tear my foot (a nail was detoured in the sun
An hour ago) but if it bleeds
I do not know, I cannot see in the dark;
The stream may be red or white or the old flood
Forcing twin obsessions into the sea
Or up the traffic'd gangplank to the ark.

The storm is gone from the ceiling;
God is not there;
I cannot comfort him, say 'let beards be'
Or smile and shave him when I cannot see.

Half-way home or where?
Fingers burn as brassy knobs rebuke them;
The key is grown, is heavy and
The python, patient, waits, across the corridor;
He does not hurry me;
We struggle, never touching skin to scale;
The end is at my door
My own two hands move docile to my throat
I choke, I splutter 'Hands!' I call them off;
I chide them, whine 'You trespass, Hands, take care!'
But they are deaf
Or death is shouting and they do not hear.

The Puritan

The earthquake's shock
Has cut a new grey Puritan
Whose ear refutes the lily note
For clank of cloven.

He cleaves to rock
And shaded stone, esteems the dark
(Excepting fireflies civil light
And stars' old spark).

How rough his word –
' 'Til they have bread I can't approve
The cherry snow, so soft so close
Is white to blue.'

Cool is his bed
And warm, so he must ruffle it
With hate; his scorn takes to a stone
To ease whose fret?

His rutted frown
Projects a whip to shrivel those
Who over ten admit the sap
That rushes them;

For blood has mown
The fields and laps the wheat in red –
'Is mine not crusted yet from seeing
Others bled?'
(Hot is the loaf that chokes the throat
That's in his head)

But still the song
Sings straight into his drum
And white the cherry floats
Though it is wrong

(Did devils deck it there?)
And still his bed
Is cool and warm and sap
Climbs up his stair
And fireflies light him home
At night, all unaware.

The great winds

I'll tell you why the great winds trouble us:
Once upon a briny while ago
The sea was home and land lay sunning, cliff
And cove and dune a-doze
In unproved element of air;
A gale ago the ocean granaries
Ran low in the sea one harvest season,
Foes swam surly through a hedge of friends
And Sea Lords fought for each sea-stalk of pasture.
One among them, Marco Polo
Swimming low in shallow water, slid to shore;
He conjured solid land, he raised a flag,
A lung, our pledge to plunge from a still water
No more moving of a mother's womb.
Each birth repeats the first howled breath in time,
Reversing all the levels of the world
Till seas come up on land,
Submerged in you and me; in bog and swamp
Released, they sing amphibian noel.

The great winds trouble when a summer storm
Breaks, blowing waves from hiding, drowning
Land-baked puff and pride in childish seas
Till we're unbeached, awash,
A native-stranger in contrary gardens;
Green and liquid shutters dim the sun

Where coral builds pink cities on the sand;
Little horses chase their tails
Among a maze of cockle shells and silver-sides
And sea-cows, udderless,
Hung, tethered to the herd by tongue-tied bells.
Here flotsam is the sloughed-off memory,
Delirium or octopus or clue
To beat the walls of water in escape,
Though tentacles are ours, were always there
Growing in the harvest of our hair;
Here sharks, all lazy but their teeth
Come swimming sweet and slow, the easier
To you know what, my dear;
And tiny barnacles that love too much
Stick, clinging till their millions anchor us;
Here mouths are raw, are filled with sorrow, washed
With salt by shocked sea-silence when we scream.

The great winds trouble till a winter storm
Breaks, frosting brine to flesh and wrecking
With a breath our web to earth;
And long before the wind's cried out
We're bound in six cold feet of Arctic ice;
No leaway anywhere to move as in
A glass-walled room, and nothing here molests
But the weight of the dying albatross
Whose two white wings lie cooling on our breast.

Time is tiger

Time is tiger.
N O W is woolly-witted lamb.
Time is tiger
(Purple shoes with crimson soles
And crimson linings deck his ears).
N O W is barefoot, black boy,
Little lost Sambo.
Time is tiger.
N O W is Mowgli, hunted, hunting Khan.
Time is tiger.
N O W is woolly-witted lamb.

Dissection

We crawl through craniums, stare
Beneath the bone at spasms, redden
At the grey twitched ultimatum when
We touch the guilty puddle where the nerve roots
Launch their tippy boats to shoot the heart.
The towering head observes which curled inch
Controls the meadow of the hand, which pipe
Dictates the course of sewers in our city;
It clocks the ragged pulse
That hammers out our imagery, unravels
Every sleeping snake
And travels to the threshold of its sting.
And while we squint to focus microscopes,
Dissect each bleeding head,
Sun bursts in splendour from the attic skull,
An angel shedding glory, come to free
The puppet dangling from a mildewed coil.

To a psycho-neurotic

You are each man's plight, distorted;
Therefore we cannot bear with you
Or the image of our near defeat
Written in black and white and pain
Across your face.
We stuff our ears against the wolf
That howls for thee and me.
We jolly you and say the sky is blue
And flowers are sweet and morning dew
A tonic for what ails the world and you.
But underneath we breathe
Your soul'd predicament;
We know the torture-chamber of the will
That 'will not',
The blanket that wraps 'do',
In 'do not',
We know the pressure of persisting
Will-rot.
We love and hate you; being us
You're doubly vulnerable –
Once in yourself, once in our lusty bluff.

Accept this truth:

You are no stranger in this rare assembly
Where the gods clutch bleeding heads

When the audience sleeps;
At worst you house an abdicated king
Who tossed away his crown.

Before you settle in despair
Listen, I pray you listen
To our voices; they are weak
But audible.

(We do not offer you child's comfort)

Two conditions of man are fixed:
The quick and the dead.
Beware the drowsy twilight bait
That lures a man from home
And traps him, traitor
In a stranger's camp.
Throw in your widow's mite,
Defend the quick,
Their victory is here and now
And will not shrink
Though they concede the ultimate defeat.

After the ballad
'Lord Randall, My Son'

'O where have you been, my baby, my son?
 O who scratched your face, my poor little one?'
'The rose tore my cheek; Mother wrap me up warm
 And hold me and rock me and keep me from harm.'

'You're bruised near to dying, my school-boy, my son,
 Your nose is all bloody; who bullied my man?'
'The girls are so rough; Mother, wash my face clean
 And stay close beside me and feed me ice-cream.'

'What makes you so sad, my young man, my son
 Who dares to refuse you, my handsome one?'
'She laughed at my love; Mother make my bed soon
 And kiss me good-night for I fain would lie down.'

'You'll not go to war, my only, my son?
 Your heart has a murmur, you're barely full grown.'
'You cut off my feet, Mother, stumps cannot stand,
 And look, they still bleed, for you're licking your hand.'

Lullaby

You'd sleep? Then come, I'll tell you where to go —
As angel or as eagle to a cloud;
Float, barely bruised, new-born, with lulla lulla
Rock-a-bye, white is the gull as the star
Is white and the snow.

But if I smother,
Breathe a feather
As a shroud?

Too soft? I know another place for sleep —
Love, shed your skin and throw your bones on sand;
The waves rest curled; they break with lulla lulla
Rock-a-bye, white is the foam as the fleece
Is white on the lamb.

But sand — the pain
From one small grain
Has drenched my eye.

You cry? A king! Awake to guide the dream!
In sleep the crown's awash, unwound the grief —
Come, cradle on your feet, with lulla lulla
Rock-a-bye, white is the dawn and the spray
Is white on the reef.

Climate of the brain

Climate of the brain, convert your Africas;
In weather white with Christmas stall creation.
Polar days wake black, and as they lock and lash
Their lid against the eyeball of the sun
So brains grow lustful for a snowy bed
Where shroudy blizzards flock their flakes, mock lethe
On budding head.

Hot hasty seed, I'd cover every sprouting one of you
With winter! There, go doze awhile
That love may hang its heart with mistletoe
Or wreathe and halo it with holly, green
And thorned and dropping blood red berries.
Season of possum death, swaddle the anxious
Seed with sedative

Till seed in-buds, digs down below the frost
And sucks at the springs of sleep.
Then, all the underworld achieved, sap
Run free at the big blessing of the sun!
What hubbub in the meadow, cock a doodle dawn
When skull ablaze with golden flowers
Fools the April morning.

THE

HANGMAN

TIES

THE

HOLLY

1955

One or three or two

Who has the cunning to apprehend
Even everyday easy things
Like air and wind and a fool
Or the structure and colour of a simple soul?

New laid lovers sometimes see,
In a passion of light;
A man, alone,
Perfecting his night vision
May be struck by dark
And silenced into sight.

But lovers sign false names
Unless their love is fable;
A man, alone,
Is unapproachable;

The dome of his observatory
May cap a hill
Or crouch in the wind of prairie
Who can tell?

Or whether far away is near
And blocks our view
Or if one joined to one
Makes ONE or three or two?

43

'I *was born a boy,*
and a maiden, a plant . . .'

'*I was born a boy, and a maiden, a plant and a bird,*
and a darting fish in the sea' – EMPEDOCLES

I live in only one of innumerable rooms
When I damp the fire with purposeful breath,
Stare at ash, sharpen
My pencil on stone at a cold hearth

Or flick the dust on good white genesis of paper,
Flocking the air with rhymes for death, soft
As the fluff of sleep or witched by broom-
Sticks, rough with rattle tall tales of bones.

Yet always I huff out the flame with breath as live
And green as Irish grass, recalling the gills
Of my youth when I was a miner
Deep in the hills of the sea.

I was a poet then. Boldly I carried my light
Through all the pressure of black water.
My blood was cold with fire for I swam
In the glimmer of a self-ignited lantern.

And I was born a boy for I bore a boy
And walked with him in the proud
And nervous satrapy of man –
Though who can hide the accent of a mother tongue?

And I was a maiden all forlorn
A long long time ago.
But the time for maidens is said to be brief
And I do not remember it otherwise –

A time of bells, with the crystal
Tinkle of grief
To indicate the supersonic moment
Pitched an octave higher than the heart's belief.

And I was born a plant. My lettuce life
Was sunny as the leaf is green.
I linger still in daymares of my flowering era –
If I blazed no light, I caught and held its sheen,

Tangled the moon in man, submissive in my flora.
For mine is a commonwealth of blood, red
And sluiced with recollection. Portage
From the sea is in the salt of my sweat,

My roots are running with the juice of stems
When pale for home they grope for a touch of earth.
Boy and maiden meander through the dendrous veins
Of everyone under the sun

But who has been a bird?
Featherless our pilots know their mammoth stretch
Pinned precarious to naked skin.
What child, from white verandah steps

Heaving his gravity with angel faith
Has not cried his tears on concrete
And on concrete learned
His kind has no primeval right to wings?

Empedocles presumed Olympic Sire;
Out of a Goddess by a God.
Beside him put his peer,
The man who stands, knowing he swam in mud.

The pressure of night

The pressure of night is on her.
She lies stiff against her saviour sleep.
Vicious as a scratch her cry
'I love the light, I'll have no traffic
With the nigger world of night.'
And her white flesh creeps.

But night is, and blazed with eyes.
Night has no shudder in
Its whole dark hemisphere of skin
And night replies
'I am your shepherd lover,
Root of daisy and the seed of clover,
I am the poet's pasture.'

But she lies dumb
Ice and fire die tepid on her tongue
Scorched with cold, the unbeliever
Resists her saviour.

Lens

I

The poet's daily chore
Is my long duty;
To keep and cherish my good lens
For love and war
And wasps about the lilies
And mutiny within.

My woman's eye is weak
And veiled with milk;
My working eye is muscled
With a curious tension,
Stretched and open
As the eyes of children;
Trusting in its vision
Even should it see
The holy holy spirit gambol
Counterheadwise,
Lithe and warm as any animal.

My woman's iris circles
A blind pupil;
The poet's eye is crystal,
Polished to accept the negative,
The contradictions in a proof
And the accidental
Candour of the shadows;

The shutter, oiled and smooth
Clicks on the grace of heroes
Or on some bestial act
When lit with radiance
The afterwords the actors speak
Give depths to violence,

Or if the bull is great
And the matador
And the sword
Itself the metaphor.

II
In my dark room the years
Lie in solution,
Develop film by film.
Slow at first and dim
Their shadows bite
On the fine white pulp of paper.

An early snap of fire
Licking the arms of air
I hold against the light, compare
The details with a prehistoric view
Of land and sea

49

And cradles of mud that rocked
The wet and sloth of infancy.

A stripe of tiger, curled
And sleeping on the ribs of reason
Prints as clear
As Eve and Adam, pearled
With sweat, staring at an apple core;

And death, in black and white
Or politic in green and Easter film,
Lands on steely points, a dancer
Disciplined to the foolscap stage,
The property of poets
Who command his robes, expose
His moving likeness on the page.

Strangers

The juxtaposition of strangers,
Charged, when strangeness claps
A lightning recognition,
Clears the sticky senses,
Humid from a hot-house vision.

Empty of heirlooms, free
From bric-brac of identity
Their vowels pray in Solomon song
And the mongol child of grief
Dies a day in their arms;
A blaze of time that is not here
Or past or in the space to come

Till, human, they close in and crack
The abstract of the unfamiliar room.

Though iris of the eye is blind
To the death of the strangers,
Pupils see their deputies,
Lovers mocking their kind
In a game they know by head
And play with wit
Below the hiding spirit.

Swimming lesson

He found her
Tied with ropes of kelp
In shallow water.
A good Seamaritan he beached
His body, knelt and cut
The weeds that bound her to an arc
About the land's tail end of rock

Then seaward over the swell
He climbed the cliffs of spray
But braked his fins and turned
When she called over the wind
'I'll drift from shore and drown,
I'm buoyant only when I swim
In shallow water.'

He listened, drifting, while
She told a tyrant's tale;
Step-motherly with threat
Of octopus and squid
She'd bound her slavish toes
To shell and sand and pebble
Tethered by the tide
To bays about the shore.

'I float in home-eroded caves,' she sighed,
'My faint head weak
Above the horseplay,
High-capped white effrontery of waves.'
'All animals can swim,' he said,
'In the swimming season;
Children wet with birth
Remember to their dying dust
The lost aquarium of Eden.'

'Not if they were dark in the well
When they were weaned,' she answered him,
'My lungs are full, I choke
On memory of water;
I live by shallow seas
Where I can hear the landlubber
Dig the rib and soil of laughter.'

'Earthbound dunce,' he said,
And there on rock, in merman's sense,
Became her master
(He was dyed a teacher –
Not in wool
But bright in silk and nylon
To his diver's soul).

'Come,' he said, 'you'll swim
With all four fins,
You'll duck your head;
Your eyes will open on
A world of fish and flora
And our own green notion
Planting rosemary and thyme
In acres red with herring
Under a sky of ocean.'

And though she did not holy believe
She'd lost the hellfire of her disbelief
And moved, a sleeping swimmer,
As he steered her out
To where the sea rolled bass with whales
And there were no more walls.

Awash and knots away
The breakers whinnied on the sands;
Fields of moonripe seawheat
Fed by currents in her blood
Swayed to the tug and slack
Of Polar streams
On the warm gulf seam of love.

On the seventh day from land
He whispered through a crevice in the roar
'Now I'll let you go and we will swim
In fathoms deeper than the need for breath,'
And she, accepting, drowned and swam
And happily lived ever waterward.

Easter sketches, Montreal

I
South of North
Men grow soft with summer,
Lack the winter muscle
Set to tauten at the miracle;
Boom and shrapnel,
March of Easter, loud
Where guns of ice salute
The cracking god.

Vision dims where flowers
Blur the lens
But here, intemperate
The ropes of air
Whip the optic nerve
Till eyes are clean with crying
For the melting hour
When flocks of snow stampede
And rocks are split by spring
And intimations of fertility
In water ring.

South of North
Men grow deaf with summer,
Sound is muffled by the pile of lawns,
But where the air is seeded fresh
And skies can stretch their cloudy loins

To the back of the long north wind
The ear is royal pitched
And hears the dying snows
Sing like swans.

II
Where campanile of rock steeples the town
Water bells the buoy of all our birthdays;
Rivers swell in tumbling towers of praise,
Ice in aqua risen hails
The bearing down in labour of the sun.

And after sun, guards of northern lights
Stand their swords; green fires kindled
By the green shoots in our wood
Cut the natal cord,

Freeing the animal sensual man with astral
Spears of grass.
Cerebral ore conceives when pollen
Falls from heaven in a buzz of stars

And time and the rolling world
Fold the birthday children in their arms.

III

North of South
Winter is Jehovah, we
The Jobs who scold the frosty Lord
Till wings of weather
Clap the air
And crows unfrock the melting God.

On our nativity
The mellowed sun is grown,
A man to kill our father,
A sun with breath so warm
It seeds the body of our summer.

Alleluia

No fanfare of flowers
But an almost inaudible
Clatter of bells
As the last icicle falls
And rivers ride again
And warn their banks
To warn the woods
And the waking worm

Of the coming Passion of our Soil,
An oratorio rehearsed by treble birds
But bursting bass from earth. O hear
The vegetable kingdom swell
And life explode,
The sound upheaved about our ears
By cabbages and cauliflower
And the gangly stalks of fresh risen corn
And radishes newborn
And row on row of cheering lettuces
Proclaiming their authentic green.

Greek island

These male and muscled hills trace their line
Back to the smoking draughtsmanship of Zeus
And in the hollows curved about the coves
The tender olive grows
And lemon sows the air with irony,
Spicing the languor of the bridal orange.

And bees sing here and the breathing sea
Inhales the breath of flowers
And hungry children cast their nets
For a catch of gods,
Scenting, in fumes of salt and honey,
Things to come and the N O W in all things past.

In June and gentle oven

In June and gentle oven
Summer kingdoms simmer
As they come
And flower and leaf and love
Release
Their sweetest juice.

No wind at all
On the wide green world
Where fields go stroll-
ing by
And in and out
An adder of a stream
Parts the daisies
On a small Ontario farm.

And where, in curve of meadow,
Lovers, touching, lie,
A church of grass stands up
And walls them, holy, in.

Fabulous the insects
Stud the air
Or walk on running water,
Klee-drawn saints
And bright as angels are.

Honeysuckle here
Is more than bees can bear
And time turns pale
And stops to catch its breath
And lovers slip their flesh
And light as pollen
Play on treble water
Till bodies reappear
And a shower of sun
To dry their languor.

Then two in one the lovers lie
And peel the skin of summer
With their teeth
And suck its marrow from a kiss
So charged with grace
The tongue, all knowing
Holds the sap of June
Aloof from seasons, flowing.

Italian primitive

A narrow virgin droops
In newborn blue,
Lips folded in, lines following
The path of stilted tears,
Medieval mother of men
Holding in inept hands
Her little manikin.

Enamel butterfly and bee,
The polished pear, sing
Beside the bearing olive tree.

Once upon a great holiday

I remember or remember hearing
Stories that began
'Once upon a great holiday
Everyone with legs to run
Raced to the sea, rejoicing.'

It may have been harvest Sunday
Or the first Monday in July
Or rockets rising for young Albert's queen.
Nobody knows. But the postman says
It was only one of those fly-by-days
That never come back again.

My brother counted twenty suns
And a swarm of stars in the east,
A cousin swears the west was full of moons;
My father whistled and my mother sang
And my father carried my sister
Down to the sea in his arms.

So one sleep every year I dream
The end of Ramadhan
Or some high holy day
When fathers whistle and mothers sing
And every child is fair of face

And sticks and stones are loving and giving
And sun and moon embrace.

A unicorn runs on this fly-by-day,
Whiter than milk on the grass, so white is he.

A *child can clock*

A child can clock
An era on the arc
Of a day in the sun

A boy is young
When he holds the pale of dawn
Smoking in his arms,

A youth, when waved with fear
The smoke's consumed
By the climbing fire.

A man is high as noon
When he can see
Ahead to trees whose shadows

Lie in sleeping dragons
On the lawn
Or easy turn and touch

The shrinking shade
Where morning
Withers on the grass

And he is old when
Counterclockwise into clown
He tumbles on

The dial of earth
And dying blows a puff
Of dandelion

Envy greens his eyes
As the flighty seed
Soars then falls to birth

The red and the green

Here, where summer slips
Its sovereigns through my fingers
I put on my body and go forth
To seek my blood.

I walk the hollow subway
Of the ear; its tunnel
Clean of blare
Echoes the lost red syllable.

Free from cramp and chap of winter
Skin is minstrel, sings
Tall tales and shady
Of the kings of Nemi Wood.

I walk an ancient path
Wearing my warmth and singing
The notes of a Druid song
In the ear of Jack-in-the-Green.

But the quest turns round, the goal,
My human red centre
Goes whey in the wind,
Mislaid in the curd and why of memory.

Confused, I gather rosemary
And stitch the leaves
To green hearts on my sleeve;
My new green arteries

Fly streamers from the maypole of my arms,
From head to toe
My blood sings green,
From every heart a green amnesia rings.

Items of chaos

On a Tuesday quiet road
A bird flew into my windshield;
By a barley field
A bullet broke the glass; a toad
Lived all its summer in a bird's nest;
A storm escaped the cloudy throat
Of a man possessed
And thundered round the town.

A Monday murder under a lilac tree
Gained a short renown
But only because the flowers
Tumbled, purple, down
Bewildering the sense
With fragrance
Poured on a common crime.

A twoheaded boy, Sunday born,
Made the news this week.
About his single neck
Authority has hung a disk,
Identifying and abstracting grief.
The father drives a truck,
The mother is mild
And knows not why from wither

Or the double hunger
Of her two-faced child.

Some say goblins. Others swear
A ring around the moon
When she conceived her son
Bewitched the way of genes.
The moon has no opinion,
The father's pride is broken,
Doctors are no wiser.
'Variations from the norm
Are plentiful,' they say,
'But not explicable.'
Sabbath voices drone
'In the sight of God, ALL
His works are beautiful.'

Tigers know from birth

My bones predict the striking hour of thunder
And water as I huddle under
      The tree the lightning renders

I'm hung with seaweed, winding in its caul
The nightmare of a carp whose blood runs cold,
      A crab who apes my crawl

My lens is grafted from a jungle eye
To focus on the substance of a shadow's
      Shadow on the sky

My forest filtered drum is pitched to hear
The serpent split the grass before the swish
      Is feather in my ear

I've learned from land and sea of every death
Save one, the easy rest, the little catnap
      Tigers know from birth

Dirge

Who killed the bridegroom?
I, said the bride,
With a nail in his pride,
I killed the bridegroom.

Who killed the bride?
I, said the groom,
I fashioned her tomb,
I killed the bride.

Who saw them die?
I, said the ice,
In my cold embrace,
I saw them die.

Who caught their blood?
I, said the sea,
It ebbed back to me,
I caught their blood.

Who'll be chief mourner?
I, said the fire,
I'll mourn for desire,
I'll be chief mourner.

Who'll carry the coffin?
I, said the wind,
Till the two poles bend,
I'll carry the coffin.

Who'll toll the bell?
We, said the lovers,
For all whom love severs,
We toll the bell.

Miser's grace

What amputation
Of the sod
To hack it out
To stretch the dead

How angular
We make the snow
When putting down
The bones we knew

A miser's grace
To fill with lead
The breathing earth
That gave us bread

Topsoil to the wind

We have mislaid ourselves, purposely
As a child mislays a burden;
As if in miracle of treason
Pastures willingly
Threw topsoil to the wind.

We gnaw the forked and brittle
Bone of wish and call it food,
Party every hour to murder
At the altar of our adulthood.

In aisles between the graves we waste
The landed fish, our flesh.
Our hearts, unrisen, yield a heavy bread.

Pastoral

Let the world go limp, put it to rest,
Give it a soft wet day and while it sleeps
Touch a drenched leaf;
Roll a stone where the skin's aware on your palm,
Stretch long and latitudinal on sand

And smell the salt drugged steaming of the sea,
Breathe sudden shock,
Drench the flesh in fonts of memory

Before you turn
Uncurl prehensile fingers from the tree,
Cut your name on bark, search
The letters for your lost identity.

On a bench in a park

On a bench in a park
Where I went walking
A boy and girl,
Their new hearts breaking
Sat side by side
And miles apart
And they wept most bitterly.

'Why do you mourn,'
I asked,
'You, who are barely born?'

'For gold that is gone,'
Said the girl,
'I weep distractedly.'

I turned to the youth,
'And you?'
'For what I have not gained,' he cried,
'Possessing her
I lost myself and died.'

And so we sat, a trio
Tuned to sobs,
And miles to go
And miles and miles apart

Till they, amazed
That one as old as I
Had juice enough for tears,
Dried their streaming eyes
To ask the cause of mine.

I told of the grit I'd found
In a grain of truth,
Mentioned an aching tooth
Decayed with fears
And the sum of all I'd lost
In the increased tax on years.

They yawned and rose
And walked away. I moved
To go but death sat down.
His cunning hand
Explored my skeleton.

South, north

Countries where the olive
And the orange ripen
Grow their men
On slopes unpuritan;
Joy a food
Deserving rites of measure.

Where winter pulls the blind
A bliss as keen –
On native stone of sin
Cold men whet their pleasure
Cussed by the black north wind.

I *am so tired*

I am so tired I do not think
Sleep in death can rest me

So line my two eternal yards
With softest moss
Then lengths of bone won't splinter
As they toss
Or pierce their wooden box
To winter

Do not let the children
Pass my way alone
Lest these shaking bones
Rattle out their fright
At waking in the night

Christmas Eve

Close as brothers are or breathing
I am tied to men whose mourning
Wears out benches in the park;
My shadow mates with shadows
Where they trespass
On the fenced and guarded acres of the heart.

They stack the litter of their discontent
On private property.
I order them to pick up skin and go
But sit and stare
When, paper thin, they stand on cardboard feet
And ask me, 'Where?'
We shake our heads and scald our eyeballs
In community of tears.

Then one among them speaks,
'Tonight is Christmas Eve;
Tattered and torn my tongue,
My heart is hanging
On the ill will of a thorn;
But if my head can rob
A neighbour of his joy
I'll be a thief of feeling,
Steal his love and wrap
A red, illicit toy.'

A felon speaks,
'Tonight is Christmas Eve
And derelicts are bitten
White with grief.
But look! enchanted children cry
To see the blizzard blacken
Where the flakes come tumbling
On the evil in my eye.'

The chorus sings
'Tonight is Christmas Eve,
What shepherd guides the sheep?
The saviour in our sinews
Is he dead or only nodding
Out his forty winks of sleep?
Noel Noel
Hullo goodbye
The day salutes goodwill.'

Terror strains my mercy
And I yell
'Go home before I call the . . .'
'Madam, home is where we die,'
They grin and sigh,
'And we can die as well as not
In your walled garden plot.'

I shut my eyes and build my hands
In dikes about my ears
(I am the priest the church the steeple
All the people
Riddled with the peak and mob of fear);
I sing song in my head,
'Tinsel angels guard my bed,
The house is warm,
The witch is chained to the barn,
God rest us merry gentlemen.'

Carol

I was a lover of turkey and holly
But my true love was the Christmas tree
We hung our hearts from a green green bough
And merry swung the mistletoe

We decked the tree with a silver apple
And a golden pear,
A partridge and a cockle shell
And a fair maiden

No rose can tell the fumes of myrrh
That filled the forest of our day
Till fruit and shell and maid fell down
And the partridge flew away

Now I swing from a brittle twig
For the green bough of my true love hid
A laily worm. Around my neck
The hangman ties the holly.

Little men slip into death

Little men slip into death
As the diver slides into water
With only a ripple
To tell where he's hidden.

Big muscles struggle harder in the grave.
The earth is slow to settle on their bones,
Erupting into mounds or sprouting flowers
Or giving birth to stones.

And how to stand a tombstone
With the ground not quiet yet,
And what to say, what not to say
When moss is rooted and the stone is set?

On *the death*
of a young poet

How can an old man
Talk with the young?
The weight of his secret
Stops the pulse of tongue

The young are saying
Men die too soon
Who die while their words
Uphold the noon

The young are grieving
A young man's death
An old man knows
Whom the gods bless

When wound is fresh

When wound is fresh
She bathes in blood
To cleanse the pain

Then fragile mesh
Of sentient skin
Shuts pulsing vein

Day after day
The graft, o thin,
Is grief to touch

So strange the way
Of healing
She wonders why

This convalescence
Calls itself relief.
Now scar is thick

Her tongue, compulsive
Hunts a redder
Wound to lick.

Daily the drum

'If we had a keen vision and feeling . . .
it would be like hearing the grass grow
or the squirrel's heart beat,
and we should die of that roar
which lies on the other side of silence.'
GEORGE ELIOT

I

Daily the drum is burst
It is not only or foremost
The din of squirrel hearts
Or the spangled noise of grass
These are simple sounds
Like bird love,
Not the sounds we die of.

II

On the other side of silence
I can hear the bones
Of bold and trembling girls
Clacking castanets
In dance of fire and fear

And who is deaf enough
When young men cry
And hailstones break the panes
That glaze the lovers' eye,
Or terror's tin scream rises,
Not from a throat
But from the key that locks
The sickness in the mouth?

The service at our graves
Comes clear, and bells,

89

But who can bear
The hidden grinding mirth
When etiquette conceals
The date and nature of our death?

And every hour a child's
Black coal of trouble
Picks at the poet's ear
Sharper than any other,
For child and poet wind
A one-day clock. 'N O W,'
It strikes, 'N O W is forever.'

These are the sounds that murder.

Boys and girls

Boys and girls come out to play
In air, in water;
All together duck, dive, somersault,
Push the waves about as if they owned
A cool blue liquid fortune;

Then, mysteriously,
For no one gives a signal,
They climb the ladder, throw
Their spongy selves on silver dock.
The pale boards darken round their bodies
Where the water runs.

The plumpness on the girls is new
And not yet of them;
Awkwardly as the farmer's boy
His Sunday suit
They wear a flounce of hips,
The prickling breasts.
Their minds have gone away to sleep
In a far country;
Nothing is, except to tease
And nurse them into women.
They do not speak to boys unless to jeer,
And sit apart,

But out of the corners of their eyes
They look at them incessantly.

Boys are proud, groin
A phoenix, fire and ash
And new-found agony;
Minds are here, not stars away
And fine nerves sing
Like wire stretched from pole to pole
In a prairie wind;
Nowhere are they cradled
In a warmth of fat
So they must tremble, boast,
Insult the lolling maidens,
Girls they hate
Whose bodies swim in their veins,
Whom somehow they must touch.

Mysteriously, again,
For no one gives a signal,
It's water time.
Pink girls rise and run, sticky
As foam candy at a fair,
Shriek and mimic fear
When the crowing boys push
Into the quivering lake
The girls they'll kiss next year.

Three poems about poets

I

Poets are fishermen crying
'Fresh catch from sleep,
Fresh as the mackerel sky
Or a salmon's leap
Is the catch we offer.
Come buy, come buy!'

II

Poets are cool as the divers who wander
The floor of the sea;
Their eyes are aquariums, swimming
With starfish and stranger.

Dark waters breed the phantoms
They haul in their nets to the sun
And sun is the power
That glisters their scales with meaning.

III

Poets are leapers, the heels of their sprung feet
Clearing the hurdles of sleep.
See how they run! Muscled with rhythm
And fleshed fair and rosy with vowels.
They're pulling the tunnel out into the light,
Did you ever see such a sight in your life
As three new poems?

Letter to my children

I guided you by rote –
Nipple to spoon, from spoon
To knife and fork,
And many a weak maternal morning
Bored the breakfast hour
With 'manners make the man',
And cleanliness I kissed
But shunned its neighbour,
Puzzled all my days
By the 'I' in godliness.

Before you turn
And bare your faultless teeth at me
Accept a useless gift, apology,
Admit I churched you in the rites
Of trivia
And burned the family incense
At a false god's altar.

If we could start again,
You, newbegotten, I
A clean stick peeled
Of twenty paper layers of years
I'd tell you only what you know
But barely know you know,

Teach one commandment,
'Mind the senses and the soul
Will take care of itself,
Being five times blessed.'

For Dinah,
the Adeneys' cat

Thirty elongated seconds
By the sun
We stared, the cat and I,
Strangers, cool and crouched
Behind unwinking green

Till flick
Along the spine, a whip
Of recognition cut
Our masks of fur and skin,
Cat o'nine tails with a sting
Neither hinted at
By curl of lip
Or spitting tongue.

Then one cat turned
With poise of air
And washed a spotless paw,
The other took a tortoiseshell comb
And almost yawned
As she combed her tatless hair.

After great shock

I. PHYSICAL FINDINGS
In slow motion body moves,
Fingers clumsy as a brood of thumbs,
Legs on the loose and stumbling
And the voice crying
'O dear why should this matter be.'

Thigh and shin burn blue with bumping
Stove and desk and angles of the dead,
Lips move awkwardly as young
And unloved girls,
Elbows swell, broken
On confusion of banged doors;
Tears dictate their gush and their withholding.

No ink yet graphs the movement of the heart.

II. PROGNOSIS
If tissue shrinks and head, aloft once more
Pilots the body, proud
Between its world of matter,
A poet's point will trace the trough
And pitch of pain, a cardiogram
Abstracted from the shaken centre.

Virginia Woolf

Her coral remnants lie
Where fishes keep their watch by night
And move transparent fins
In hollows of her delicate drift-bones.
From ivory pelvis spring
Her strange sea changeling children;
In sockets deep with six lost layers of sight
The sea fans open.

Poem in three parts

Those behind me
Those about me
Millions crowding to come after me
Look over my shoulder.

Together we consider
The merit of stone
(I hold a stone in my hand for all to see)
A geologist tells the time it has endured
Endurance, a virtue in itself, we say,
Makes it own monument.

We pause, resent
The little span
A miser's rule
Inched out for man

But blood consoles us
Can be squeezed from us
Not from stone.

Saying this fools no one
A sudden bluster of words
Claims for human seed
A special dispensation
Foxes and flowers and other worthies
All excluded.

99

Immediately sixteen creeds
Cry out to be defended –
A state of emergency exists;

Flying buttresses
Revolving domes, a spire extended
By the spirit of
A new and startling growth of thorns

Skies in Asia catch
On uptilted wings of temples
In the Near East the talk is of stables.

11
Above-below the din
A few quiet men
Observe the cell's fragility

How Monday's child
Makes Tuesday's vegetable
And Wednesday petrifies
The leaf to mineral
While Friday sparks the whole in fire
And Sunday's elements disperse
And rise in air.

III

The stone in my hand
IS my hand
And stamped with tracings of
A once greenblooded frond,
Is here, is gone, will come,
Was fire, and green, and water,
Will be wind.

Twilight of the gods

One man prayed
'Hold your nuclear Sun
On the Right hand of heaven,'
Another cried,
'The God of Power belongs
On the Left hand with the chosen.'

As was to be expected
Neither received a reply.
But how could they admit?
Forging God's signature
Each sat down
And composed a holy writ.

The two books were so similar
They might have been written by brothers;
For absolution both proposed
Last rites, flood-lit.

To a sleep addict

Turn your compass from
The point of sleep.
Let the fixed pole wait.
Why hurry the traveller home?

The track is short so beat
The racing blood
For when its foaming dries
No whip can make you bleed.

The linen that covers us
At last, is cold and worms
Are hatched in shadows
Of our human arms.

Speak now

For we must hold our peace
When resurrection springs
From the crook of an ulna
And slithers through the grass.

Where cliffs, reflected, cower

Where cliffs, reflected, cower
I see the image of a stranger
In a sheltered pool.

He clings to crumbling
Ledge and the clatter
Of three pebbles, loosed and tumbling,

Drowns the edgy grief
Of fingernails and the torn quick
Pleading for his life.

I hear him sigh. Fatigue lets go
And up he comes, though he comes crashing down
Where hawks are crowned, and kingly

Feed on the delicate ways of flesh
Then sharpen jaded beaks
On a jag of bone.

Below the clouds but far
Above his head the hawks are lagging.

I would cry my heart around
And stretch it to a wide red net
To catch the falling stranger in.

I'd hold him still and stunned
But safe from vultures and the titter
Of small birds

Waiting for his thud
Of matter on the ground.

But my red boasted net
Is less than air, the mesh
Too weak with words

To bear his weight
Or frighten off the plunge
Of preying birds.

Shorn of grace
I stare at the mocking pool
And throw a stone

To break the image of his fall
And my cold face
And the white gull bearing our souls away.

POEMS

FROM

PERIODICALS

AND

ANTHOLOGIES

Nature be damned

(uke)

I

Pray where would lamb and lion be
If they lay down in amity?
Could lamb then nibble living grass?
Lamb and lion both must starve;
Bird and flower, too, must die of love.

II

I go a new dry way, permit no weather
Here, on undertaker's false green sod
Where I sit down beneath my false tin tree.
There's too much danger in a cloud,
In wood or field, or close to moving water.
With my black blood – who can tell?
The dart of one mosquito might be fatal;

Or in the flitting dusk a bat
Might carry away my destiny,
Hang it upside down from a rafter
In a barn unknown to me.

I hide my skin within the barren city
Where artificial moons pull no man's tide,
And so escape my green love till the day
Vine breaks through brick and strangles me.

III
I was witch and I could be
Bird or leaf
Or branch and bark of tree.

In rain and two by two my powers left me;
Instead of curling down as root and worm
My feet walked on the surface of the earth,
And I remember a day of evil sun
When forty green leaves withered on my arm.

And so I damn the font where I was blessed,
Am unbeliever; was deluded lover; never
Bird or leaf or branch and bark of tree.
Each, separate as curds from whey,
Has signature to prove identity.

And yet we're kin in appetite;
Tree, bird in the tree and I.
We feed on dung, a fly, a lamb
And burst with seed
Of tree, of bird, of man,
Till tree is bare
And bird and I are bone
And feaster is reborn
The feast, and feasted on.

IV

Once a year in the smoking bush
A little west of where I sit
I burn my winter caul to a green ash.
This is an annual festival,
Nothing to stun or startle;
A coming together – water and sun
In summer's first communion.

Today again I burned my winter caul
Though senses nodded, dulled by ritual.

One hundred singing orioles
And five old angels wakened me;
Morning sky rained butterflies
And simple fish, bass and perch,
Leapt from the lake in salutation.
St. Francis, drunk among the daisies,
Opened his ecstatic eye.

Then roused from this reality I saw
Nothing, anywhere, but snow.

Variations on a theme

I

There is always a first flinging
Of the blood about in circles,
A falling down, a sickness ringing

In the ear, a swivelling eye
Uprooting tree whose tendrils flower
On sagging skin of sky.

Green blades cut, they spin so fast.
Round and round, a child on grass
Whose name in anagram is lost.

II

I turned round once; I shut my eyes;
I opened them on truth or lies.
And this is what I saw though
Cannot say: or false or true.

From arteries in graves, columns
Rose to soil the sky; and down
Their fluted sides the overflow
Slid to earth, unrolled and spread
On stalk and stone its plushy red.

Trees had shed their limbs, become
Mobile marble guards. Secret

Their manœuvres in this land;
And while they marched a mad dog's tooth,
Rabid violet, tore half my hand.

The wind blew from the south
Before I turned, but here a north
Wind blew, and I was lost. It blew
A milch cow dry, a new moon down;
Then higher roared until it blew
Seven fuses of the sun.

III

We shut our eyes and turned once round
And were up borne by our down fall.
Such life was in us on the ground
That while we moved, earth ceased to roll,
And oceans lagged, and all the flames
Except our fire, and we were lost
In province that no settler names.

IV

I shut my eyes and turned once round;
I opened them on alien air;
Sea had shrunk to farmer's pond
And sky was pink and distance near.
A forest and its nights were now

113

Woodpile for an old man's fire;
And where above me one black crow
Had cawed my spring, two dirty doves
Sang daintily. I stoned the birds
But no stone hit, for of white gloves
My hands were made; I stole a stick
To break the sky; it did not crack;
I could not curse – though I was lost,
Had trespassed on some stranger's dream
Where swan forswears his lust,
The gull his scream.

v
I shut my eyes and turned twice round;
Once for death, once for love.
I fell down twice upon the ground
But what I saw I cannot prove.

Death turned me first. When he had done
Black rings moved about the sun;
Love turned me next. I fell to rest
In quicksand, and was quickly lost.

Death turned me first, will twirl me last
And throw me down beneath the grass
And strip me of this stuff, this dress
I am, although its form be lost.

114

A *cautionary tale*

> '. . . *we had sold our death* . . . *for the sum of* £*70* : *18* : *6d*
> *and lent our fear* . . . *on interest of* £*3* : *10* : *0d per month,*
> *so we did not care about death and we did not fear again.*'
> — FROM *The Palm Wine Drinkard* BY AMOS TUTUOLA

She met a lion face to face
As she went walking
Up to her hips in grass
On the wild savannah.
So close they stood they touched
If she put out her thumb
Or he his soft ferocious paw.
She bore no weight of fear,
For only yesterday
She'd leased it to a rich man, poor
In that commodity.
Without her terror she was free
From the alarming smell
That irritates a lion
And makes him lash his tail.
And so he yawned, and stretched
On the long stemmed grasses,
And in the pouring sun
She sat beside his royalty
And sang to him a tale of moon.
Before he rose to go
He opened wide his jaw
And took between his teeth
Her wishing bone, as if to say,
I could, you know.
A rich man had her caution

So she laughed; cool,
In the lion's ear, her pretty breath.
What happened next happens
To every maiden fair
Who lends her fear
But forgets to sell her death:
The lion ate her up, and down
To the smallest crumb.
Lord have mercy upon
Her sweet white bones. Amen.

Falconry

'*The* Boke of St. Albans *had laid down precisely the classes
of people to whom any proper-minded member of the Falconidae
might belong. . . . The list had defined itself meticulously downward
to the kestrel, and he, as a crowning insult, was allowed to belong
to a mere knave – because he was useless to be trained.*'
– FROM T. H. WHITE'S *The Goshawk.*

I

Eagle for an Emperor
Peregrine is due an earl
Goshawk is the right of yeoman
Kestrel for a knave or no-man.

God's left hand must bear them all :
Eagle of the emperor,
Peregrine that's due an earl,
Yeoman's goshawk, and the knave's
Bating kestrel, no-man's slave.

Rather bating kestrel, I,
Than mind the fist beneath the glove.
I, a kestrel, God, the Knave –
And I will bate[1] until I die,
And bite the leather of my jesses,
And starve before I eat His messes.
Can I do more? Sweet Knave, I'll try.

Yet that fist and glove are home,
For, banished, what could I bate from?

[1] To beat the wings impatiently and flutter away from the fist or perch.

II

As falcon on a falconer's wrist,
So should I, on God's big fist;
Yet will I not or preen or sit
Or take His lure, the rabbit skull,
And dip my hawking beak in hell.
Rather would I bate:
Head-down hang and scream and squawk
And churn the air and rough my feathers,
For though the leash that holds my jesses
Ties me to the precincts of His glove,
I will not love.

If tidbits do not tame His falcon
God remembers Babylon
And proper ways to tease and starve
The lust upon His leather glove.
Regard me now; I quiet sit,
Brooding on the skulls I'll split.
Or watch my flight; its easy pause,
Angle of incidence inclined
Against the bitter wind
Before I dive, 'God's mercy in my claws.

Notes on Robert Burton's 'The Anatomy of Melancholy'

SIMPLES

To damp the fire that burns in Billy
Extract of the water lily.
Man who eats a cabbage quite
Can drink and not get drunk that night.
If falling sickness trouble you
Down a glass of Dutch sundew.
Your lungs are clogged? Kind Sir consent
To hyssop, horehound, calamint.
If head's at fault, then betony,
Or sage or rue or peony.
Should stomach prove the house of pain,
Wormwood, sorrel, and purslane.
For liver's yellow melancholy
Decoction make of agrimony.
Finger-fern and maiden-hair
And a dodder of thyme the spleen restore.
Kidneys clear for those who swallow
Parsley, saxifrage, and mallow.
Mugwort will the womb renew,
And pennyroyal, and featherfew.
Hearts on roses fed grow calm
With borage, bugloss, basil, balm.

AMBER AND SPICE

If the brain be cool and moist,
Amber and spice, amber and spice.

But should the brain be hot and dry
Amber and spice will your wits away.

CONSIDER
THE EXCELLENCY
OF VIRGINS
Virginity, a pious picture,
So said holy Bonaventure;
Blessed state, and meritorious;
Rare like all things virtuous.
Take John the Baptist – chaste in bed –
He chaste remained, yet lost his head;
Or Daphne, maid of some renown,
Who to a green bay-tree is grown.
And Joan (she but obeyed the voices)
Burned, and not in fire of roses.

Married folk replenish earth,
Virgins die a striking death,
Married folk are wondrous wise,
Virgins people Paradise.

CHELIDONIUS
Rave no more, go find the swallow.
In his belly is a stone.
Lap that stone in leaf of willow,

Wear it on your mad right arm.
O how you will merry merry be,
And all your sorrow gone.

PAUL

A pint of honey, a gallon of gall,
A dram of pleasure, a pound of pain,
An inch of mirth and an ell of moan –
What more do you want, asked Paul.

A gallon of honey, a pint of gall,
A pound of pleasure, a dram of pain,
An ell of mirth and an inch of moan,
And less of your preaching, Paul.

DEATH

Death himself, when he had stroken
With his dart this fair young virgin,
Doted, yet his trade being murder
He must be her cold clay's lover.

Day or night he could not leave her.
Death is dead, said one believer.
Rigor mortis flapped its arms
And no mouse died, or beasts in barns

Till Death of Love at length grew sick,
Put on his cloak and went to work.

POST MORTEM
Empedocles cut up a corpse
And this is what his knife reports
On one who, doting, died of love:
Liver, smoky as a stove;
Brain, a cheese; the heart, combust;
Lungs, a sneeze, a pinch of dust;
And soul, not yet returned to God,
A suet, maybe, or a sod.

NEPENTHES
Polydamna's gift to Helen –
Nepenthes, a tranquillizer.
Such its virtue that if taken
Steeped in wine, says my adviser,
Though Trojan lovers drop down dead
Helen smiles, and goes to bed.
This happy weed I know for certain
Is but borage. So says Burton.

SOCRATES
Socrates was merry by fits,
Sang and danced and shook his wits,

And with his children he was known
To ride-a-cock-horse in the Parthenon.

SON OF JOVE,
CHICK OF HEN
He was light, and sprung from Jove,
She, the chick of a white dove.
The moon from envy loosed her hair
And caught these two in a silver snare.

She took them for an awful ride,
Even showed her humped backside.
Son of Jove, Chick of Hen –
You fare no better than mortal man.

DEVIL
Devil, being slender spirit,
Enters by the nose or gullet;
Couches, cunning, in the bowels,
Shakes and frights our shying souls.
Devil of our fearful dreams
Is, and *is* not what he seems.

THE CHASTE
AND THE UNCHASTE
Persons who from venery abstain
Offend fair Venus – virgins who complain

123

Of vapours, migraine, and black melancholy –
Chastity's reward and virtue's folly.

Intemperance she deems an equal sin.
Old man, young bride, hot summer – can he win?
So parched and shrunk is he from chamber work
He must go mad, or leave love for a book.

A gallon, Burton says, of moistening remedy
May ease a ravaged rake of his extremity.

NUN
She did not sign it with the cross –
That tender lettuce leaf;
She nibbled without thought to grace,
And Devil is a hungry thief,
And piteous her horrid fate:
Garnished nun on Devil's plate.

Mark you, those who have the wit –
Ne daemon ingredi ausit.

POEMS

FROM THE NOTEBOOKS

Letter to my children:
Postscript

With winter here my age
Must play with miracles.
So if I grant you wishes three
Scoff and say I owe you five,
Five full and fathomed senses,
Precision instruments
To chart the wayward course
Through rock and moss and riddles
Hard or soft as ether, airy
Airy quite contrary
Where will the next wind blow?

With sense alive you're wiser
Than the man who ploughs the profit
From his field
For you, a child, still touch
Taste, smell out heaven and hell
When lying hidden
In the waves of wheat his acres yield.

I'd set your heart by relativity,
With space for slow and fast,
Set five alarms to wake and catch
The shadowless noon
Before it moves to after.

And luminous be thy dial
To read the pale
Gold numerals of dawn
Thin on the face of the midnight watch.

Your kingdom comes with senses
Schooled to top professionals;
The ear, a master bred on dissonance
Of urban sound
Will mark the drop in pitch of towns
Adrift in fog
And the lowering of evening song
When the strut is gone
From the tenor birds;

You'll shiver but you'll hear
The sharp white nails of the moon
Scratch the slate of midnight water;
Your ear will share
The loneliness of curlews crying,
Record the laugh of loons
On the delicate grooves of madness.

Before you tar with age
Swing to hot percussion jazz
Of insects, dance

To carnal charivari
Broadcast from distended throats of frogs.

And when the windy autumn blows
Hoist antennae, gather
The blazing brass of your being
To compass the ocean's scale
And crescendos
Surfed from a sea in storm.

When waves go limp come home,
Push the water in your bath and echo
On a porcelain reef
The older swell and foam;
Adjust, as seamen do on land, to gales
Blustered from a gutted shell
On a parlour mantel.

Uncage the tiger in your eye
And tawny, night and day,
Stalk the landscape for the contour
Of a fern or arm,
Gorge on pigment squeezed
From barley fields
Or part the strawberry leaves

That hungry eyes may water
On the fruit and feast of colour;

Let eager pupils measure
Girth and bravado of bulldozer,
Watch the flex of iron muscle
When giant shovels
Grind their jaws and roar,
'Like Samson I can lift a ton
Of terra in my teeth.'

Speed your vision till it follows
Power and plumb of a bullet's line
From gun to heart,
Slow your eyes with patience, see
The bud relax-
ing as the petals yawn apart.

Touch everything available
To consciousness,
Birch and bark of cedar, tables
Worn to silk by women
Rubbing their restlessness
To polished wood;
Shut your eyes and feel a way
To linen and lover, marvel

At aluminium, cold in the sun
And at the thermossed fire
And chill of stone.

Touch worms and warts
In gratitude for shudders, stroke
The soft white bulge of peonies
And trace their crimson veins
Back to the milky memory of mothers;
Sharpen wit where nerve ends
Lace the skin of fingers –
Their tips will clock the pulse
Beat of a leaf –
And when by some enormous morning grief
You are undone,
Feel the warm salt water
Where your eyes swim, green
With childhood
In the last sea vestiges of home.

And with a scholar's nose
Catalogue the flowers
Fighting for precedence in June,
Learn the lesson
Stinked at you from skunk or drains
And from pot pourri of

131

Department stores inhale
The current substitutes for love;

Smell the vigour
Packed in snow at noon and metal
In the air
When stars show up for duty
On the dim lit wards of winter
And breath is everywhere white with veils
And the vows of nuns.

Taste a thesis on your tongue,
Honey, lemon, spring sprung water
Loaded with geology.
Skin and flush of peaches, red
Tomatoes picked and bitten in the sun
All gush the juice and seed of summer
To the learned mouth.

And sense how prehistoric fathers
Weigh our modern cells with jungle genes
When huge our appetite for lean
And fat of meat
Sets saliva dreaming of the kill
A million years behind the nearest hill.

In milk and curd of cheese
Guess the whey and whyfore
Of our interval need of peace;
For bread and wine
Let wisdom on your tongue
Pause to conceive a fivefold grace.

'Sleep well' – I wonder why
We harp on sleep, our certainty.
I'd turn the message inside out
And have you listen
With immaculate ear
To what the bells of matin say,
'Wake well, my child,
Don't lie on your nose,
Today is a holy day.'

Roches Point

This land rings,
In stone of its houses,
In cedar and sod,
The myths of my kin.
The long lake knows our bones;
Skin and scar and mole, sings
Them like a lover, truly.

Here eternity lit
On sunburned shoulders
Till seven cat-black summers
Stalked each other and us,
And for our terror
Deadly nightshade
Flowered in our wood.

The body still goes back
For of necessity
It makes strange journeys.
I, my being,
Shut the door against return
And in the attic pack
One hundred summers,
Seven burning wounds,
A root of deadly nightshade
And the silky waters
Where our epochs drowned.

Indian givers

The sea came to call on my mother and gave me my blood,
But the Old Man left a warning: tell her, he said,
Not to forget the flood.

The mountains called on my mother and gave me my bones.
They shook themselves and rumbled of fiery stones,
Of Etna and fiery stones.

The earth came to call on my mother and gave me my flesh.
A troublesome thing, she said, not worth a wish,
But I crowed at my pretty dress.

The heavens called on my mother and formed me a skull,
Stuffed it with mist and with clouds from a nearby hill –
Indian givers, all,

    For they will be back:

    The sea for my blood
    (Once I quite forgot the flood),
    The mountains for my bones
    (Twice I laughed at fiery stones),
    Earth for my flesh
    (Thrice I tore this crumpled dress),
    And heaven to crack my skull
    And claim its clouds, three bags full.

Ballad

An old moon mutters a dirge on my pillow,
Mother, O Mother,
The sun dropped dead in a cross of blood,
And my shadow wears a cobra's hood.

My hand is cool on your cloud white brow,
Daughter, my daughter,
Dawn will drain the sun of blood
And stop the old moon's mutter.

But what is the name of my fear,
Mother, O Mother,
Why is a cobra coiled round my soul?
Why does an apple make me ill?

If wishes were kings, I'd grant you sweet dreams,
But wishes are worms.
Spit forth the apple, drop the serpent
Hissing in my guilty arms.

Rhyme

A mother nags her daughter,
'Beware of Dick and Harry.'
O why should she nag her daughter
When she herself was merry?

A mother begs her son
'Be chivalrous with maids,
But if they be not maidens, O
Take to your heels and run.'

And boys and girls bow low, bow low,
'Thy will be done,' they say
Then hang their clothes on a budding limb,
'Be quick, my love,' they pray.

Nursery rhyme

Under the sky is a tree
Under the tree is a stone
Under the stone is the grass
Under the grass is the earth
Under the earth, the small white bones of a child

Under the sky is a tree
(And grown since I was here)
That marks the stone
(And colder than I remember)
That marks the grass
(And surrendered to weed)
That marks the earth
(O mother earth indeed)
That hides the fine white dust
Of a child whose small white bones are lost.

Whose murderous shadow, then?

We stand in my oasis, Black and White,
And tell our times of day.
He, the dark one, strikes the jungle noon.
A desert clock in the pale of his palm
Is sand that will not wait my sifting glass.

I, the fair, the o so innocent,
Hide bloody hands behind my back,
And say, I guess white time of day is dark,
And unto our sons, except their skins, no light.
What could I do? What have I done?
And blood from my fingers falls on a stone.
He smiles, a sickle moon on the face of night,
And I regard his darkness, now so gathered up
It leaves no smallest shade on the summer ground.
Whose murderous shadow, then, butchers the grass?

[The tightrope]

High as fear
The tightrope,
Thin as silk the string
My feet are walking walking
Since my mother cried
And the doctor cut the cord
And stranded me here.

Numberless as clowns
Are my beginnings –
Teeter, crazily totter,
Windmills for arms;
The long street breathless
And I more breathless than windows,
Waiting.

But I am two times born
And when a new moon cuts the night
Or full moons froth with my
And witches' milk

I walk the tightrope
Free and easy as an angel,
Toes as certain of their line of silk
As the sturdy ones
Whose feet are curled on earth.

Effigy

He did not recognize Jehovah,
Allah, Zeus,
Apollo, Eros, Dionysus,
Or Pan who scuffs the tidy turf
With an itching hoof.
Nor did he hear the little
African gods in the drums of their people.

Other men might knock on wood
But he'd no use for charms,
Abracadabra was nothing to him;
His silver never crossed a gypsy's palm
For he held his future certain, and his fortune.

Only in sleep (a child can sense
Something is in the dark to be avoided)
Did he admit them and cry out
'I pray the lord my soul to keep;'
The next night he might thrash and shout
'The devil's got me.'

One evening he came home to find,
Pinned through the eyes to his front door,
An effigy.
His likeness stared, personal
As marble, and as solid.
He looked, and laughed; and choked, and died,
Murdered by tears he could not weep.

March, April, June

The month that pocks the earth with scabs of snow
With my blood rhymes;
The juice that navigates the veins of trees
Tours all my trunk, explores my slumbrous limbs
And in my ear a hush awaits the crow.

The sun that kills with kindness failing ice
Heals wounded faith;
An upstart shooting green above the ground
In my bed shoots and buries shoddy death
And on my pillow moons and April kiss.

This June that takes the city to her breast
Is my year's dower;
As lovers rushed with sap relax their thighs
At bursting excellence of fire in flower
So am I burst by sun, and sired my seasons rest.

I *was witch, or skilled magician*

I was witch, or skilled magician,
Squeezed three aspects into one,
Or stretched one into three;
Changed myself to bird and leaf
Or branch and bark of tree.

In rain, and two by two, my powers left me;
Instead of curling underground as root and worm
My feet walked on the surface of the earth.
And I remember a day of evil sun
When clumps of green leaves withered on my arm.

Now, like any deluded lover,
I curse what once I blessed, for I was never
Bird or leaf or branch and bark of tree;
Each is separate as curds and whey,
With signature to prove identity.

Yet still we're kin in appetite,
The tree, the bird in the tree and I:
We feed on dung, a fly, a lamb,
And burst with seed
Of tree, of bird, of man,
Till tree is bare
And bird and I are bone,
And feaster is reborn
The feast, and feasted on.

Slade's cloud

'It's a cloud,' he said.
'A head in a cloud –
A cloud in a head –
But a cloud,' he said.

'No, no, it's a head.
A misty old head of an old sea man
But a head,' she said.

'The man in the moon
Is the moon
And the head in the cloud
Is the cloud;
I know,' he said
'For my head's in the clouds
And the moon's in my head.'

[Old Adam]

My old man had a rib in his side.
It was his sorrow and his pride.
I took it from him while he snored.
In his dream old Adam roared,
And when he woke he wept to see,
Of pride and sorrow I'd made me.

Adam's rib

Ring, without beginning, end;
Spire, the thrust t'ward heaven's round.

Angels bright rotate, encircle
Urgent tip of god-in-steeple,
As on earth all Eves inquire
The nature of the rib they were.

Adam and God

On Monday man gave God
Dominion of the sky;
On Tuesday swore Him
President of waves;
On Wednesday crowned
Him Emperor
Of every creeping thing,
A monarch of the night
And King of day;
On Thursday
Man breathed into God
Man's anger, charged His gun
That God might fire from heaven;
On Friday
Bade Him eat the apple, fallen
From the Good and Evil
Tree in Eden;
On Saturday
Man grumbled, 'God
Is lonely, has no peer
To share His fate'
And cut the Devil
From a sleeping woman's rib;
On Sunday
God cried, 'Rest! Enough!'
And ran from man and hid.

Leda in Stratford, Ont.

A silly country maiden went
A mile or so to Stratford, Ont.,
And here she found, as everywhere,
Things much too ordin'ry for her;
Yet from a Richard, Rex, or clown
She learned of Leda and the Swan,
And so admired their high-class union
That up and down the banks of Avon
She ogled those immaculate birds
That never turned to take her crumb
Or listen to her honeyed words
Of love, but simply swam.

A crow, observing her odd wish,
Laid the girl beneath a bush;
No sudden blow – the great wings beating –
More as a joke, a kind of larking.
And yet she doted on his action,
Tickled by such rare seduction,
Boasting to the birds, 'Black Swan,
Demon Lover urged me on.'
But no bird listened, for a caw,
Loud and rude, came from the crow.

Noël

She begged a blessing from the snow,
Cool, of pity clean,
In rose, and in a bed of straw
Where the lamb had lain.

She hunted God by the light of the moon,
She wore a hedge for shirt;
The holy river ran off with her sin,
And she ate a leper's dirt.

But leper died, and the hedge was torn,
And homeward ran her sin.
Frost and thorn, and mice in the barn,
And God in a tiger skin.

A bright star led to a palace of gin
Where all the queens were tarts,
And kings were toads, and crowned each queen
With coronet of warts.

The barman there was quick to tell –
You'll here no grace discover,
For toad and tart embrace one hell,
The heaven in each other.

149

She entered, and she saw instead,
Rose cuddle with the toad,
And lamb and tart in a bed of straw
Asleep beneath the snow.

Shadow and substance

'Niggers say a drowned man's shadow
was watching for him all the time' — FAULKNER

With stick, a string, bent pin,
A bit of worm,
More often than a trout,
He hooked his shadow in the lake
But never landed him.

Later, in a distant stream,
With burnished rod and burning reel,
He cast for salmon, fished the river
Dawn till noon, but never
Raised his image from the pool.

He sailed a ship upon the sea.
Below the swell his buried face
Regarded him, but never rose,
Or muscle moved when sly shark bit,
Or curlews, screaming, dived for it.

One winter night the rain fell down;
It puddled every street.
Everywhere he walked his shadow
Licked the soles of his halting feet.
It could not wait —

And why should he?
Give? or take? so it be done.

In gutter water's soiled embrace
The two were one, then gone –
No tattered shade, or bite for worm.

Divining rod

A freezing rain has frozen my forked self
And my forked hazel twig.
Hazel twig was my green god, I,
The obedient child. It pitied me my thirst
For when the mouth went dry
There it lived in my hands and by its tremor
I was led to where the water ran.

But I am no longer a dowser.
Divining rod lies still in my lax fingers,
Even over deep wells;
Wood that waked at the touch of my green thumb
Now will not leap or shake the sockets of my arms
To tell me holy, holy, here the spring runs.

Boastful songs

I

When I wake up with all my feathers primed
And ready for the moon
Who then outflies me?
A million million million?
I never stop to see, am totally
My wingspread and my speed, and poems
Pouring from my pinions as I dive.

II

I feel the fine ridged sand against my belly
Here, in shallow water where I lie
Beside my love and make my boastful song.
It praises us, our silver scales, and suns
That rise, not in the east, but from our loins.

[*If you should die*]

If you should die
I'd give my flesh
For purposes of worms
And ivory grow my bones
And moss my hair

Until I grew desirable
To death
And you moved over
And we shared the earth

Summer storm

Morning is more still
Than a long pause
Stretching awkwardly across the room;

Wings are waxed from flight
The mourning dove laments on rigid air
A whistle splits the atmosphere
  Skull's skin is paper thin
  Migraine is seeping in.

  Then ailing day
  Blows aerial jibes
  At rooted earth,
  Rumours fly
  From wave to wave
  Puffing omened gusts
  At ruffled looking-glass.
  The panic'd leaves
  Rattle soft green bones
  On agitated trees

Orchestrated heat from katydids
(Tropic tom toms with a northern beat)
Press on nerve ends in the brain
(Migraine seeping in again)
Blindness blocks the naked lighted night
Eardrums plug with fear of loaded guns.

Zigzagzip

Zigzagzip
Cat o'nine tails whip
The tender night
To splintering applause.

Unicorn

I went north to read heraldic spoor,
Passing on my way, Muskoka, motor-
Boats, motels, and at the Georgian Bay
A snake beside its skin. No unicorn.

Someone said its horn had last been seen
By moonlight on the northern shore
Of Lake Superior,
But the only white thing there – a whistling swan.

So I came home, empty, quite in despair,
Opened my black door and shook the rain
From my good eye, and moon
And unicorn ran down my tumbling stair.

A *room for sleep*

Muffle the vibrato in my room
And wash the air with plain-song;
Stage must fade to white
And white go out in grey
                    and I in sleep.

No scarlet here,
No trumpet from the noisy sun;
He'd blow the shadow of a dream-set
To oblivion;
In this cave, let white
Shade into grey
And grey black out and I
                    black into sleep.

For props, bring downy doves;
Their monotone
Proves violet a gaudy, rose
Another name for hussy (roses
Point a thorn
Then publicly unpetal all they own);
Lilies are not here
Or swans, for would their pride
Let white be smutched with grey
                    that I might sleep?

Ring the curtain
On the opera in my room,
Wash the air with plain-song;
Shake a snow-storm
On the ruff of dozing dove
Till flake is leagued with feather,
White and grey, till black
                    strikes twelve o'sleep.

Waking

A long long long time later
Than the day I was a child
I woke from watered sleep
And I was heavy-hung with salt,
Caked all about with cockle shells
And dried sea smears;
No flicking fin's
Last fling at salmon's leap
But a yawn as I turned and stretched
From the drowning years;

I pumped my lazing lungs with air
And rubbed the sea away and tried my legs
And shook the snails from my hair;
I dug with a curious hand on my first sea-shore
To a pool where a pebble ring'd the long salt swim
And drowned my new-found crying in its roar.

[If I *could here insure*]

If I could here insure my soul
I'd not insist on cash at death
Or Florida rent free
Eternally.
I'd take a policy for living accident;

The soul drops much too fast
In elevator shaft or shoots
Too vertically strung
For wings from ground to sun
(A membrane slivered thin
Needs balanced tensioning);
It bogs in sticky sleep that glues the eye,
In wax that blocks the drum from noise,
Melts for the wheedling voice.

I'd settle for my soul's wit wide awake
And gamble on the night to bring me sleep.

Amphibian shores

Eyes stretch across the land
Blink at fields
Up from the bottom of the sea only yesterday.

We cry 'A house!', choke,
A thatch of sea-weed is green-growing roof
We focus on a half-remembered wood, boast
The latin name for the immediate tree,
Stop, confused – a star-fish on a limb!

Is this our land? Crust and crab and wet
Anemone? The sea-horse neighs, faint
For the salt-soaked weeds of home.

Our hands hang thick with barnacles; toes
Curl soft and wary on a coral path;
Tongues trip on vowels, taste a changed saliva
When we know the hill but see the grass
Blown counter to prevailing, off-shore wind,
Stems anchored to the tide
Waving to its wide pre-natal hymn.

Laced in foam we sway, fall,
Pray cognition in cathedrals, chant

A Plain-song in their surf-vibrating shell;
We breathe a World with round Amphibian Shores
Where the lung adheres to the gill, the skin to the scale,
Where the heart, warm, wrapped in moss, rests on the horn.

Fishwife

Friend, this green aquarium
Where we, perforce, are dumb,
Drives us to drink. The plankton
Here's too salt, and we too wanton,

Yet can do no earthly thing,
For though you're whole, a man, I'm not
Myself below the waist; petered out
In mermaid – see, I fling
A scaly hip, a fantail ending.

Round and round we swim, lament
My fishiness, our discontent;
Then, what you've been waiting for,
I lash my tail against the floor

Of our green tank. Down you dive
(O sinuous predicament!).
And quick with jumping silver knife
You slit my tail, that we may love
Without impediment.

Fallout

Noah, God denied you sun;
Forty days His anger fell.
Now, in His own image, man
Makes the gentle rain to kill.

And what we know? is what you guess –
Noah, hear the father-wish:
Punished loin, the punished bone
Burn again in punished son.

Seared by dewdrop, or small rain,
Ark, we'll enter, one by one
Lest man or creeping thing or bird
Multiply from fallen seed.

Death in America

As sex was once, now Death is gone
From decent persons' conversation.
Neighbours cut him in the subway
Though underground he rules the country.

Yet name him not. Death now is IT;
Glutton, lecher, hangman, heel.
Have you heard? Young Dan Jones –
Yes, poor thing, of D – – – – appeal.

Hide IT black beneath the covers
Where lie hidden other deaths,
And when the van comes, and the movers,
List these mysteries as births.

Investigate, subpoena the rat
And he, not you, will grow in fat.
Yet, could you cast him out, who else
Has dark horse to pull your hearse?

Storm

First, a storm that ripped the rooted growth of trees
And tore the skin of love off the palm of the hand;
Next, a decade when the rain dropped straight,
No wind to point it, rain dropped swords on the land;
It bathed the birth from lambs where sheep lay weighted,
Roped with rain-soaked wool; it fell where trees
Were lying weak and drowned as violets
When stem and stamen clog with grounded bees;
It splashed where herds of eagles strained to lift
A host above the earth's humidity;
It raked the sockets, steeped the bone,
Each weeping pin unstopped a sutured vein
Till hearts gushed out in clots and ran their banners
Down to the stream and the streams bled into the sea.
When land was clean,
An Eden, by sun forgiven, seven seas were red.

[I *never see a stone*]

I never see a stone
Without an inward groan
And feel again the impact of my race.
For should I chance to peer beneath
Its smooth and granite face
I see no other
Than a brother
Come crawling out with looping squirm,
Wet, white and eyeless, fellow worm.

A *sorrow of stones*[1]

1. SONG

In this graveyard, hedged, they lie,
A lady and her gardener.

On windless nights they rise and see,
Across the hedge, the high corn grow,
And appled moons on apple boughs
And petit pois all in a row;

Never bleeding heart or lily,
Or the pink, black-centred poppy;
Gone the wind's anemone.[2]
More than sun and rain they sought,

Not by rain and sun alone –
Petals pocked with brown and blight
Died of love one summer night;
In the rosebed, tree of stone.

2. STONECUTTERS

I

He works methodically, slow,
Chips at stone; grave hands, grave mouth;
And this his solitude: each blow

[1] Country saying for a graveyard.
[2] Anemones are also called windflowers.

Breaks the skull and dugs of myth.
Stone in hymn endures, and yet
Stone is subject to his flint.

Plumb he cuts and fits the rock
Of ages to a garden walk;
Or dates it, stands it upright on
Grassy roof-top of a tomb.

II
Down to pebble, now, or chalk,
Stone by daily weather worn.
Dwindles rock to grain of sand,
Waits the coming of new land
When promised bubble breaks earth's rind
With hurricane of granite wind.

3. PENELOPE

The turf she strokes above his head
She spins into his hair and beard;
Her fingers sieve the soil and rush
With quickening of their common flesh;
Stone becomes (her hand on stone)
Sweet and pact of marrow bone.

And thus the gay grave-loving nun
Whose lenient Lord has bidden her
This fitting habit, husband, wear,
Sits beneath the spreading sun
And pays no heed, cuckoo, cuckoo,
To bird or man, so she be true.

4. WHEN A BODY BREAKS

I

When a body breaks or is
Cast off from its hemisphere
Something grave has gone amiss.
Danger, danger, everywhere.

Moon broke loose, or was she thrown
Altar high that none dare doubt
Her powers, now more potent grown,
As Helen's have, with chant and rhyming?
No man puts to sea without
Her tides' consent; and at her waning
Virgins pale, and bribe with moon-blood
Goddess of their maidenhead
Whose light can stone or warp a womb
Or send the lovers mad.

II
It happened on a Tuesday, noon
(A body breaks or is cast off),
And being neither moon nor Helen
I fell down a well,
Commonplace abyss,
Black and waterless,
And in the falling turned to stone.

I shot through earth; now am come
Right back where I started from
In outer space,
Our point of genesis.
A tunnel travelled indicates
Some kind of birth, a milky way,
But not to me; my mouth
Is stone and sucks on meteors.

Twinkle twinkle how I wonder
What I'm falling from up yonder.
Virtue? Vice? Abstract nouns?
If vice, it is my sloth, my own,
My slug in hiding under a stone
But not under me anymore
For I am on all sides exposed
And falling down,

On through graveyards where the dead
Stars lie cold, their glitter gone.

I hail white Jupiter.
God-white Jupiter, I call,
But he is king and need not stare
At stone, except in monuments.
Venus combs her copper hair
As I come plunging by,
And Mercury, the slippery one,
Talks to redfaced Mars,
But none of them talk to me. O
Try another tongue, cry *Marduk*
Ishtar Nebo Nergal.
They pay me no heed as I drop,
No more than Sin and Shamash.

It is other than I had imagined. I thought
To travel behind two plumed white horses,
I thought to lie like cream in a long black hearse
I had not calculated on this
Fall without end.

[By *word of tongue*]

Burst the skin off the tongue
Till words reflect a hotter sun
Than ever shone in heaven;
They'll fright the devil's tufted ears
And shrivel hawthorn's holy spears.
Be done with comma and the groping guess
And hurl a brick at words like loneliness;
No good to wish our language new –
Spell words that spit at need of dew.

O take a chance at jungle mating;
Verbal tigers' progeny
Will sever eye and ear
From garden grown endeavour.

An endless, glutton's feast of words
Is waiting the releasing yeast,
The working curd.

[Accustom the grey coils]

Accustom the grey coils
Locked in the skull
To the silence, then knowing
Seeps in through the bone
To the dungeon, no telling
Except to its dwelling place,
Shadowed cell cluttered with
Tales left unfolded.

Listen, you grey coils
Locked in the skull,
To the pounding; it's growing
As fontanelle shuts
On the silence; the swelling
Predicts at its pressing point
Hoarded night bursting, the
Black sky unloading
Its stars till the skull is alight.

Confession

I know so well what I want to say,
I even know some of the words
And the rhymes that wait to translate it.
And then I begin – and begin – and prevaricate –
I hedge my course with blinded byways
I tunnel under lighted highways
I cannot say 'this is how it is
On the flood lit road'
And thrust my pen ping into a reality;
I buck or shy left, I suggest
A graveyard fixed in night
Rather than look an honest hour
In the face, by broad daylight.

A

PROSE

MEMOIR

Four corners of my world

LONDON

Three houses dominated our London (Ontario) world: Lornehurst, Eldon, and our own. Lornehurst belonged to our paternal
grandfather, Eldon to an aunt and uncle.

We lived within a block of Eldon in a high house topped by a
mansard roof, and owned as well the land across the road, land
that fell steeply to the flats below and the Thames River. The
family hoped that years of fill would one day make sufficient level
ground for building, but it was our good fortune to know it in its
embryonic state, there being no richer playground than the varied
layers of growing yet garbageless dump. Old tin cans, bottles,
broken and unbroken, little steel-grey mountains of cinders, bits
and pieces of stoves, the springs and stuffing of chairs – and every
week a fresh load to be examined. Once I found a pair of corsets
which I laced on over my coat, and thus adorned sat with my
Eldon House cousins among this celestial rubbish – with a rub-
adub-dub on tin-can drums, and singing 'Kelly Kelly with his
buskin belly and his ass all painted green. . . .'

Eldon House still stands. It bulges with things as a house is apt
to when the same family has lived in it for one hundred and thirty
years. The drawing-room contains seven sofas: Georgian ones and
early Victorian love-seats. It absorbs them effortlessly, as the hall
absorbs elephants' legs and tiger skins and poisoned arrows and
spears and swords, an array of fire-arms and the forest of antlers on
its walls. Moose and deer looked down on us with cold glass eyes,
eyes that had never seen a fern or tree, yet moved one strangely,
as much in their way as the eyes of live gazelles. It seemed

they spoke more emphatically for death since they had not lived.

It was a pleasure of childhood to go big-game hunting with Uncle Ronald, the killer and procurer of this treasure. We stalked our prey through the dark L-shaped hall where tiger skins rose in living cats as he guided us on perilous safaris.

The Eldon attic is an awesome place. During the past few years expeditions have tried to catalogue its contents, but progress is slow and only a small path has been cleared from end to end. But an illegitimacy has been stumbled on and countless pictures of our childhood selves.

Eldon is beautiful. Lornehurst was not, being typical of those houses built by the rich in Western Ontario in the eighties and nineties. They featured towers and were very impressive to children. We loved it for its size, the dark halls and elaborate ugliness, which did not seem ugly to us, only strange and exotic.

We often played in the billiard room at the top of the house. From here a door opened onto a stair that led to the tower. But it never opened for us. The door was locked. Years ago had someone fallen? We did not know. We only knew that the tower, our hearts' desire, was forbidden us.

My grandfather, or so my mother said, bought pictures by the yard, and for the dining-room he had chosen the likeness of a lion. Life-size it appeared to a child, and it hardly seemed prudent to eat right under its nose. The drawing-room contained the necessities of an earlier era: two fire-places, bow windows, polar-bear rugs, little sofas and little chairs; and there was a small dark 'reception room' in which no-one was ever received, and a big library where the family lived.

Our London and paternal grandfather was in great vigour until two weeks before he died, a gregarious man of whom it was said that the train trip from London to Toronto gave him the exact time necessary to extract the life history from every fellow traveller in his car. He believed (and was not mistaken) that our Toronto and maternal grandfather could circle the globe without uttering a word.

The Lornehurst stable sheltered our father's horse and Darkie, the pony our mother drove, and the electric car. The electric car was an oddity even in those days. It resembled a horseless carriage and ran (battery-propelled) at a maximum speed of five miles an hour, almost without sound. On Sundays in fair weather grandfather and grandchildren set forth in this dowager-on-wheels. The car was open and the pace slow enough to observe persons and objects with the exactitude of pedestrians. Our grandfather was a friendly man and he waved to everyone he knew and also to those he didn't. And we waved to everyone and everyone waved to us.

These family tours often led to calls on friends of our grandfather, and the most portentous of these was a journey to a sham castle where Mrs. Shaw-Wood lived with her parrot. But the sham wasn't sham to me; it was the archetype of all castles, and first glimpsed from a long straight driveway bordered by dark steepled spruce trees.

We were an hour on the way. There was something of a hill to climb before we reached the gates, and hills were hard on the electric. But arrive we did, and pulled up in front of the nail-studded door. I can no longer distinguish between hostess and parrot. They were both there but which was which escapes me. The image wavers. I would doubt its reality had I not later ascertained that such a person existed, that the castle stands there still.

ROCHES POINT

At Roches Point I witnessed my first summer, as did my mother and brother and sister; and the whole or part of every subsequent summer; hence no beginning, no moment when I observed it consciously for the first time. The place is tall with tales of grandparents, uncles and aunts, my own generation and that of my children. Under the circumstances it is difficult to say what happened to whom. As members of primitive tribes experience group rather than individual emotions, likewise our eighty Roches Point summers appear to belong equally to the dead and the living. Here time flaunts its paradox; rushes by yet never moves an inch – a caged squirrel running on its revolving stair.

When my maternal grandfather bought Beachcroft it included the main house, a gate-house known as The Lodge, and eighty acres of parkland. The nearby village was then wholly rural, and the countryside, to the water's edge, farmland or maple woods or cedar swamp; some distance still in time from Toronto and reached by a series of journeys: first by train to a point south of Barrie, then two miles by wagon from station to lakefront, and three more by ferry to the Roches Point Government Wharf. Later the grandfather's yacht, the *Minota*, carried family and visitors direct to the Beachcroft dock. And its passengers are still there, in albums and pictures: young women in high Gibson-girl collars and trailing skirts, sedately seated on its deck, no lounger among them; or on the dock in long flounced bathing dresses, black cotton stockings concealing their legs from the sun's glance; and beside them, suitors and brothers clad in garments resembling flannel underwear, yet nonetheless beautiful in the eyes of their beloveds.

On rainy days we studied these presences in family albums. Under canopies of clothes did they rejoice and sorrow? They appeared remote as pterodactyls, yet the snapshots of my childhood are yellowing too and now I feel closer to their fancy dress than to my children.

The Lodge is my mother's house and everything in it speaks of her. It wanders about in an inconsequential manner, having twice been added to. The original structure is of field-stone; walls three feet thick and floors that dip and rise according to the varying states of the sagging foundations. Here the upstairs windows are round, like portholes, our welcoming moons when we come walking home at night. The additions are shingle and the whole is comely, has a flavour that is generally admired despite its dowdy old-fashioned airs.

For many years our mother refused the conveniences of elec-

tricity, and we upheld her, certain the atmosphere would be corrupted by such city fixings. A wood stove served in the kitchen, and candles lit our way to bed, but electricity was permitted to power the pump so that our bathrooms were orthodox.

Behind the kitchen is the wood-house, but once it was the ice-house. In winter men cut frozen blocks from the lake and stacked them here, with plenty of sawdust for insulation. Sometimes on hot August afternoons my sister and I escaped the sun and sat in this cool dark tranquil place, delighting to emerge into a heat and glare made more intense by our deep-freeze siesta.

Our acres were peopled with children, and every morning at eleven we met at the Beachcroft dock to swim; big boys and girls together in a group; little boys in another, lying in a row like small bronze fish and forever shivering; and we, the little girls, kept our designated place in the hierarchy. The 'little boys' were yet senior to us. Sometimes we played together, sometimes not. We varied from year to year, dependent on those mysterious forces that work in children, alternately separating and bringing together the two sexes.

The boys had a hut, we a wigwam — secret male and female dwellings in which on rare occasions we entertained each other. The boys told us jokes we believed blasphemously obscene and we enjoyed a pleasurable sense of wickedness. But they were concerned for the future. 'You'll get pure,' they said, 'when you're twelve or thirteen.' We vowed we wouldn't, knowing the label 'pure' to be the most contemptible insult in their vocabulary. We could not visualize our future selves; nor did we understand that 'purity' is the shroud of dead innocence.

Children in books have daily adventures and we prayed vigorously to be likewise blessed. We searched methodically for underground passages, hidden caves, buried treasure, for ghosts.

Once, while walking through a farmer's field, a dozen mild-eyed cows change in a trice to a herd of charging bulls, compelling us to race for the nearest fence, hurl ourselves over, breathless with fright. Then, saved by the grace of God, we turn and see the field all quiet again, cows slowly munching.

Only when courage was high did we visit the haunted house, long since deserted and fifteen minutes distant from the village. Its windows were broken, the front door hung crazily from one hinge, half the roof had gone and weeds flourished inside as well as out. This was the last resting-place for dust, a kingdom of spiders, a paradise for bats. Half a mile away we were already fit to faint at the smallest quickening or dying of a breeze, at a shadow cast by a flying bird. Only once had we the temerity to go beyond the hall.

We are uncertain in what form the ghost moves, for it is not a well-known spirit. In fact nobody knows about it except ourselves. We climb the stairs, a step at a time. Halfway up they start to sway and swing. The stairs themselves are haunted. We whisper, not daring to hear the echo of the spoken word – then tumble over each other in our haste to get out before we too are bewitched, gone forever from grieving family and friends.

Which reminds me of another happy way a child can pass what might otherwise be blighted hours. For instance I complain at breakfast of a sore throat I haven't got, and my mother says I can't swim. No-one to play with. All the peoples of the world disport themselves in the lake, so I find a rock far from the madding crowd and the fun begins. I am thrown to my death from a horse, or killed by a lunatic driver, or I drown, far out at sea – preferably all these things – and my crumpled body is brought to my mother and laid at her feet. How she weeps, how she wishes she had been kinder to her daughter. Soon I am swimming like Alice-in-Wonderland in my own tears.

No children were more devoted to their mother than we to ours, yet such an affection in no way altered the fact that adults were enemies, not bitter enemies (except on occasions), but natural, inevitable ones. And we had no wish to change the *status quo*. Their greatest offence was in regard to Time, an abstraction they did not in the least understand. They were always ringing bells or calling Time for breakfast, Time to get out of the water, Time

for bed – whereas we, with a more philosophical concept of the clock, knew that Time, in their sense, did not exist. What we happened to be doing was forever, whether it was floating in the mild blue lake, or lying in bed, half asleep, on a summer morning. Slowly the enemy won, and thereby robbed us of immortality. Before we knew it our own hands were shaking bells and calling Time for dinner, Time to go to bed.

Children's games were surely invented by adults with the intention of minimizing the bloodshed at birthday parties. But why are they designed to make fools or outcasts of the players? Observe the tense faces and bodies of little boys and girls compelled to play musical chairs and you will know what I mean. The children do not run – they creep along beside the chairs, their anxious bottoms hovering over each as they pass. Always one less chair than child and when the music stops one is always 'out'. According to their tragic faces 'out' might as well mean dead.

And Blind Man's Buff. A man's white handkerchief is folded to a bandage for my eyes and knotted at the back of my head. Three times I am twirled about, more lost than an African in Siberia. I do not know where any thing or person is, or where I am, or in which direction I travel when I take one hesitant step forward. Somewhere in this black emptiness, which is at the same time cluttered with unknown objects, I must find and catch a person. Arms outstretched, clutching handfuls of air, I stumble this way and that. Somewhere I hear a noise of breathing and I lurch to where I think the sound is coming from. But now there are many sounds, from all directions: small whistlings, sudden hand-claps, laughter. The close one, the breather, is saved. I plunge wildly, knowing the thing I search is near at hand, yet in my blindness knowing it beyond my reach. When at last I am returned to the visual world I stare at signposts – lake, grass, house, trees, people – and I shudder, remembering the dark.

Truth or Consequences is not a birthday party game. The intended pleasure is the suffering of one's comrades; to deal out

Four corners of my world

Consequences, to listen to horrid Truth.

We played with the solemnity of field-marshals. Consequences were as dangerous as we dared to make them, or of an embarrassment more fearful than danger. He who chose Truth soon felt the turn of the screw.

'Which do you love most, your father or mother? When did you last wet your bed? D'you cry when you're spanked?' Truth is intolerable. But Consequences may mean going to an aunt's kitchen and saying a four-letter word in the presence of the cook, or walking the rest of the day with stones in your shoes. Consequences are intolerable.

We liked picnics, particularly those that took place beside a stream in a stagey-looking wood. Hard maples, cedar, beech, and, by the river, willow trees.

We called it the vanishing wood, for though our mother knew every bump of every road in the vicinity of Roches Point, sometimes it wasn't there. We attributed its supernatural nature to an old man who lived, not in a house, in nobody knew what – perhaps a cave. He was commonly known as the Owl Man and as unpredictable as his wood – sometimes there, sometimes not – and though we feared him, we always wanted to see him just once more.

Today we find the wood. When it is here it seems impossible that sometimes it is not. My brother opens the gate and we walk a short way through the trees to a clearing beside the river. The trees have not changed their positions. Thistles are real enough to scratch our legs. In the August stillness, with only an occasional cicada drilling in the dry grass, we are conscious of our voices. It is as natural to whisper here as in church – more so, for here the gods are not tamed by a human preacher.

Our mother suggests that we explore the woods, and we go, but never deep in the forest. We skirt its edges, peer between the trunks of trees – hoping, hoping not, to glimpse the Owl Man.

We are peeling hard-boiled eggs on the river-bank when he appears, is suddenly among us, an old man with hair falling to his shoulders, and a beard, bushy and decked with twigs and leaves. My mother greets him politely and offers him a sandwich. It disappears behind his beard and he begins to talk. I do not follow the words, only the strange wailings and mutterings of his voice, the oracular gestures, the eyes, wild as their shaggy brows. He is a Presence, one whose dwelling is a sacred grove which he makes manifest when it suits him to do so.

While we are driving home my mother says, 'You mustn't be afraid of the poor old man. He's quite harmless.'

Then I know the wood to be yet more miraculous than I had believed it, for the Owl Man had appeared in one guise to my mother, in another to me.

'Watch the road,' she says. 'We often lose our way going to the wood. What if we should lose it coming home?'

According to Ambrose Bierce 'in each human heart are a tiger, a pig, an ass and a nightingale'. The Roches Point general store is an emporium of vast importance, particularly to children, and once a week, when we visited it to rid ourselves of Saturday's allowance, tiger slept, ass brayed but gently, nightingale lay as if dead, pig reigned supreme.

Our wants were known and tray upon tray of various and savage-coloured candies were spread before our snuffling snouts. Four for a cent, three, and some as high as two. We deliberated, rolling saliva around our mouths with quivering tongues. Fifteen cents each, enough for a good-sized paper bag of forbidden fruit – orange and pink and poison green and one long liquorice whip. We acted against the law. The law permitted something pure like a stick of barley sugar or a peppermint, one a day.

As we could not take our loot home we must eat it at a sitting, and for these orgies we chose the churchyard. It had not then been tidied, and the old gravestones were covered with periwinkle, and where periwinkle had not thrived, lily-of-the-valley covered the mounds of the dead. Great white pines shed their needles on the flowers beside the field-stone church of which we are so fond. It was as familiar to us as the Lodge and we were forever wandering in and out of what we felt to be our private chapel. But on porcine days we remained outside; sat among the dead and the periwinkle and the lily-of-the-valley, or perched on tombstones, meaning no irreverence.

Here we talked and munched and gloated and gagged until we had downed our week's fortune. More than once my sister was unaccountably sick on Saturday night, but I do not remember losing a penny's worth.

Our Eldon House aunt and uncle and cousins often came to visit at Roches Point. They travelled in a car known as Grandfather, a patriarch already fifteen years old when it entered their service, though as its former owner found the open road not to his taste, it had not then travelled a thousand miles. It remained with the Harris family another fifteen years, a venerable monster with sufficient room in the back seat to set up a card table, and this, on long journeys, they frequently did.

The car was open and high and conspicuous by reason of its contours and great age, so when this vision included four people gathered around a card-table absorbed in a game of bridge, it produced no small sensation as it rolled through the streets of Toronto and on, north, to Roches Point. My father's family have never had the slightest objection to being 'conspicuous', unlike my mother's who suspect 'conspicuous' is kissin' kin of Satan.

London is more prone to eccentric happenings than the reticent Toronto. The case of a well-known golfer, for instance. Not a pro, just an enthusiast. After his death the mourners, gathered in his house for the funeral, found him dead indeed, though he hardly appeared so, seated as he was in a chair, his feet on a stool, a familiar figure in his plus fours, a putter clasped between his hands. Not a Toronto funeral, certainly.

TORONTO

After our father's death we lived with our maternal grandfather at Craigleigh in Toronto. I cannot recall him at Roches Point, though we have a picture of him there surrounded by fifteen grandchildren, and we are among them. During our five years at Craigleigh he never came, and for me this was a continuing sorrow.

On winter evenings I recounted its delights. 'Next summer you'll come?' I begged.

'I'm an old man, child. There are too many ghosts.'

'But it's your *home* – don't you love it any more?'

'I can love it from here,' he would answer, while I sat beside him, close to tears.

Once in mid-summer I was summoned from Roches Point for a few days' visit. Without a member of his family in the house he sagged with melancholy.

I find the grandfather sitting on the red-tiled terrace. From here stone steps lead down to the Italian Garden. Italian urns overflow with pink geraniums. In the middle is a pool where goldfish and water lilies swim, and surrounding the pool, flowerbeds are bounded by pink brick paths.

With the grandfather's help I read the time on an old sundial; then sit on the round curved edge of the pool and swish the water with my hands, wishing for cherries to eat, or plums. Instead of supper with Lizzie, the Craigleigh nurse, my evening meal will be afternoon tea with the grandfather, and a plate of something extra. I wonder what but am not hopeful. Cook does not strain herself preparing delicacies for the young.

Out of the corner of an eye I regard the grandfather. Do I only imagine that he is especially unhappy today? His welfare, once my proud responsibility, is already a heavy load. I am hypnotized. I have become my grandfather. The years of his life hang themselves on my shoulders yet do not lift the weight from his.

William and a parlour-maid bring tea; cinnamon toast, anchovy sandwiches, and fruit cake. My extra: cold, limp asparagus lying on limp, warm lettuce.

The following day my spirits remain low. I am accustomed to a Craigleigh full of people – my own family and visiting cousins and the coming and going of aunts and uncles. The silence of the big house makes a noise like a funeral march, and the acres of garden and ravine in no way compensate for Roches Point.

I talk with the grandfather and sometimes I make him laugh, and I hang about Lizzie, the old Craigleigh nurse, while she sews and clucks on about Master 'Ughie and Master Jack and my mother, Miss Mary, the perfect children of another generation. But when I wake at night, fearful of the dark, she is reluctant to share her bed with my shivering self.

'It isn't 'ealthy for a young person to 'ave an old person near them at night,' she says.

'Why not?' I ask.

'Because the old weaken the young by breathing in their 'ealth,' she answers me.

I was a sickly child and Lizzie knew the reason why. All my strength had gone into my long heavy hair. *Inquire Within Upon Everything* was her secular bible. From it can be learned manners and morals; how to conduct oneself during childbirth and remedies for every ailment.

It may appear redundant to advise a young woman to 'take off her stays' before giving birth – so an aunt thought, and laughed. But she was caught by her second baby, still laced, not even in bed. Which shows you can't mock without the gods hearing.

Somewhere among its pages is a chapter on the deportment of ladies, a sentence of which remains with me still: 'If her teeth be good she should smile but seldom, if bad, not at all.' Probably Lizzie's faith in a greasy substance known as cocoa butter came from *Inquire Within*.

In winter, after our baths, she rubbed the stuff all over me and my sister. She said we would absorb its fat and put on weight. Next came spoonfuls of cod-liver oil, or, in spring, a molasses concoction which she said would purify our blood. Hairbrushing was the last bedtime rite. We took turns in a chair before the huge nursery dresser, and there each received the prescribed one hundred strokes. I liked it when Lizzie talked about her girlhood in England, and the young German – his name may have been Albert, for I associate him with the Prince Consort – who asked her hand in marriage. Her family refused, on the grounds that he was a foreigner. What was good enough for royalty was not good enough for them.

'No-one else ever asked me,' she would end, and I could hear in her voice an unfamiliar note of wistfulness. And we would sigh, thinking of her long-lost lover.

Mrs. Bailiwick, the seamstress, came to Craigleigh for two weeks in the spring and again in the fall. She made our clothes, and no matter how charming the pattern, the finished products had the Bailiwick cut, a sad cut. Droopy. My mother believed that a simply dressed child was a smart child. In our Bailiwicks we proved the exception.

The sewing-room contained, as well as the sewing-table and an old-fashioned sewing-machine, two portly dummies – headless, billowing creatures who prepared me for modern sculpture – so obviously female without in any way resembling a woman. They appeared to have a life of their own and I never equated them with inanimate objects like chairs and tables.

It was at these I stared while Mrs. Bailiwick pinned up a hem. She was a thin, blotchy-faced woman. To enjoy her company it was best to breathe through the mouth, for she smelled of bad teeth, old sweat. Cockroaches, I believed, clung to her armpits. Lizzie muttered dark warnings in regard to her sanity and we had no reason to doubt her.

'Stand still, hold your arms down, turn when I say turn.' Mrs. Bailiwick is on the floor, a yardstick in one hand. A hundred pins tremble in her mouth. 'Mad as a March hare, my husband was,' she says, and a little gush of pins fall clink clink clink on the brown linoleum floor. 'Feel safer now he's gone. I was getting supper one night and he hits me over the head with a raw beefsteak, and the bone in it too.'

'What did you do?' I ask.

'Got out my pinking shears and pinked him good.'

'Where,' I asked, 'did you pink him?' How well worth her smell is Mrs. Bailiwick.

'That would be telling,' she answers, chuckling like a witch, and the pins drop from her mouth, clink clink clink on the brown linoleum floor; not plain linoleum – linoleum bordered by pink roses.

My brother knows everything. He is never wrong. If you bet with him you're sure to lose.

Most of the time I am proud of his infallibility, but on a dull winter afternoon he is right once too often and I bop him on the nose, knowing it to be his Achilles heel and knowing he is not permitted to hit girls.

A quicker intelligence would have foreseen that he would pin me to the floor and bleed a red Niagara all over me, head to toe. When the job is done to his satisfaction he gets up without comment and goes to wash. I lie still, stunned by the sheer beauty of his revenge. When I hear Lizzie's approaching footsteps I close my eyes. She looks down on what must surely be the victim of most foul murder. I open my eyes. 'Alan's nose-blood,' I say, and Lizzie's face relaxes. She forgets her anger in the glory of the bath and scrubs unmercifully while I, in a marble tub encased in mahogany, pretend I am afloat on the Red Sea.

I was almost fourteen when my grandfather died. Craigleigh had been torn down more than a year before I returned to what had become a city park, a portion of the original property.

I stood where the house had stood and tried to build it up again in my imagination, brick by brick. Nothing happened. It was as if I had gone to a looking-glass expecting to meet my own image and had found no self reflected back to me. Green grass grew over the labyrinth of cellars. Green grass carpeted the floors of what

I had believed to be eternal rooms. In vain I papered the air dark red, as were once the walls of the long wide hall, but it would not hold, nor the pictures in their heavy gilt frames. And the curving stair kept tumbling down. Yet time has returned it.

Now I can hang the curtains, even flick the dust on a corner of the nursery dresser that Lizzie's failing eyes so often missed.

I am in the morning-room with the grandfather, a cosy, shabby room. On the bilious green carpet many small oriental rugs appear to have been spread at random, but there is no random about it. Each is carefully placed to hide a hole.

English linen, overblown roses, faded leaves cover the comfortable, clumsy chairs. The grandfather's chair is on one side of the fire-place, and on a table beside it the Egyptian cigarettes he smokes too many of. There is a chaise-longue on which my mother lies.

Nowadays the grandfather seldom goes beyond his gates, and he is restless. So am I. He stubs his cigarette, groans a little, gets out of his chair, cusses his legs, and I know we are going to walk from room to room, examining pictures, reading the titles of books in bookshelves, talking. Talk I like best, but it takes strategy to get conversation from the grandfather.

In the hall I first admire his full-length portrait, then turn to the worst picture in the house. It is very large, and entitled 'The Story'. A lantern lights the face of story-teller and listening boys. It turns the straw in the hayloft to Rumpelstiltskin gold. The rest is shadow. I sigh at so much beauty. But when I ask the grandfather's approval, he only grunts and says, 'The boys' faces are too clean,' careful not to altogether smash my love. Nonetheless doubt creeps in. When other children admire it I say, 'Except that the boys' faces are too clean, it is perfect.'

On the opposite wall two Raeburns hang, side by side, man and woman. The man has a red nose and a red velvet cap on his head, and the woman wears what I believe to be a wimple. They belong now to the Toronto Art Gallery, and sometimes I salute them there. I like the man best but the grandfather says the woman is more valuable, and when I ask him why he tells me that given equal merit a portrait of a woman always fetches a higher price. I am immeasurably pleased at his reply.

Next we shake our heads over an eighteenth-century portrait of a young man, a glamorous fellow, but one whose eyes, the grandfather says, have a shifty look. I half expect him to mend his ways under our censorious stares, but he remains invincibly a rogue.

We leave him and regard the sturdier qualities of ancestors: great-grandmother's olive skin, compassionate black eyes, cap that ends in a froth of lace falling to her shoulders, almost a mantilla; great-grandfather in black clerical coat, and, above the dog collar, a fair, bluff face, cleanshaven except for white sideburns; great-great-grandfather, an eighteenth-century man with a sensitive, perhaps querulous mouth; great-great-grandmother in an elaborate bonnet edged with a deep ruche of lace, a big satin bow fixing it beneath her determined chin; finally great-great-great-grandmother. She had been Joan Drew, sister of Samuel Drew, the 'Cornish metaphysician', before she married Edward Osler. Her bonnet is organdy, and its delicate frills contrast oddly with the straight thin mouth and the eyes that seem to say, 'If you'd seen what I've seen you'd keep your mouth like mine, tight shut.'

The grandfather sighs. He looks a long time at the portrait of his mother. Because she lived to be a hundred we always think of her as a century, not a day more or less. Once she walked these floors, a living presence. Her footsteps are still everywhere heard.

The grandfather opens the shiny mahogany doors that lead to the drawing-room, a room of grey brocade and spidery chairs, a room abandoned since the grandmother's death. Over the fireplace hangs a portrait of a young woman by Hopner. Not so long ago she looked down on balls and At Homes and the changing fashions in hats. Now the room sleeps. Nothing ever happens here. Yet in this dormant room lies my little prophet.

He lives, along with other curios, in a small glass cabinet mounted on a table with elaborate curling legs much encrusted with ormolu. It is not permitted to lift the lid unless you are the grandfather. He tries to interest me in a jewel-handled dagger, a hunk of jade, Marie Antoinette's inkstand, but I see only the infant Moses, gold, and tinier than my little finger-nail. His mummy box is half an inch long, enamelled in purple and red, and lined with red velvet. Hinge and clasp are of gold. The grandfather puts this trinket in my hand. (After his death Moses became mine, but the god, removed from his temple, without the ritual of the opening of the glass case, or the grandfather's presence, ceased to be important. Later I found his likeness in every Cairo bazaar.)

The grandfather puts Moses away and we move along to the library, a great-dane-lying-on-the-hearth sort of room, a bit majestic, yet so warmed by books and the three-foot logs burning in the fire-place and the blaze of flowers in the conservatory that it appears more lively than its inhabitants. Here the pictures are mostly Dutch, brownish, and full of grazing sheep. Only one is strange – a picture painted by Monticelli when he was mad. I look at it more intently than at any other picture in the house, believing it will tell me what madness is.

There are no pictures worth speaking of in the billiard-room so we head for the dining-room where the grandfather pours himself a whisky and soda to which he adds a dash of angostura bitters. Angostura bitters, a few drops, he shakes on the back of my outstretched hand. I lick, absently, hardly aware of this so-long-established custom. (We move through the house, repeating our gestures like dancers.)

The dining-room gives the illusion of being round. The east wall is windows, ceiling to floor, and gently curved. Pillars grouped in semi-circles cut off the right angles of the other walls. The effect is Toronto-Roman. Togas would not here look out of place, or bishops, or robber barons. The table is round, the chairs are Chippendale. Highland cattle from the security of massive frames regard our Sabbath eating of roast beef.

CALIFORNIA

I lie beside my mother shivering still from the nightmare that has brought me to the shelter of her comforting presence and the flowery smell of her bed. The moon shines on the sea. I listen to the soft murmur of surf breaking on the sand. The shivering stops. I sleep.

When I wake salt mist spiked with mimosa and eucalyptus drifts through the open window. I would lie here forever, sniffing, but breakfast is ready – porridge, boiled eggs, toast and marmalade and milk. My brother and sister know the dark has deflated me once more, and when I sit down to eat, they say, 'Scaredy cat!' I stick out my tongue, then start to blow on my porridge.

After breakfast I watch the sun dissolve the last wisps of fog. Little lizards appear from nowhere and lie on rocks or on the pebbly paths. I try to tame them but, indifferent to my overtures, they scuttle away when my hand comes close – swift as humming-birds or still as sticks – stiller because the beating heart in animals when they 'freeze' makes stillness absolute.

Bambooland – for such is the name of our house – is situated five miles from Santa Barbara on a spit of land between a single railroad track and the sea. It is always for rent when we want it, perhaps because it is shabby, perhaps because three times in every twenty-four hours a train seems to roar through the kitchen. But trains are a small price to pay for a view of bay and mountains, and a garden ending in a cliff and a wide hard sandy beach, golden in colour.

Yee is our Chinese cook, and like Bambooland he appears to belong to us. Some winters we come to California and some we don't. We never let him know in advance, yet he is always waiting for us and for his kitchen where the pots and pans rattle when the train roars past.

Every Thursday afternoon he goes to Santa Barbara to gamble and smoke opium. On Friday he gives us a box of lichee nuts, his smiling face a little more so or a little less, depending on his luck at the table and the number of pipes. He treats us with gentle kindness but is none the less aloof, a member of an ancient race with no small talk for barbarians.

Sukey acts as housekeeper-nurse and comes with us from

Canada. Wilson, the chauffeur, also comes from Canada, driving the car across the continent while we travel more prosaically by train. He sings bawdy songs, though not in our mother's presence, and has a fat and frequent laugh. From cowboys he has learned to do tricks with a lasso, and it is a pleasure to watch the ruddy-faced Canadian and the fine-boned Yee snaking the rope on the asphalt outside the garage, absorbed in their sport and content with each other.

One day my mother asks my sister and me if we would like to go to school and we say 'Yes', not having been. There is a small day school near by run by three Canadian women which our brother already attends. The classrooms are hardly more than big verandahs, and each has a stove in the middle as protection from the early morning cold or the rainy season's damp. Not that I remember cold or damp – only golden sunshine playing on feathery pepper trees, on olive, on shaggy eucalyptus, on the coarse fans of the palms, and on orange and lemon and lime. I remember praying for rain when a drought set the mountains on fire, but I don't remember rain at all.

Walking home from school one day I am happily bursting bubbles of tar on the noon-hot road when a fellow-pupil turns to me and says, quite casually, 'My fourth Daddy is coming home today.' I stare at her in astonishment but she appears unconcerned, as if four fathers in seven years are the norm, not three too many. When I tell my mother, she explains, vaguely, divorce and the marital exuberance of Californians. Our own father's death becomes of a sudden an honourable loss, and though our mother is continually courted, I see no reason why she should ever remarry. After all she has us and surely we are plenty.

We have miles of empty beach to explore. One day a girl whose father knows our mother joins us where a cluster of rocks is exposed, for the tide is out. She has freckles and is older than my sister and I and therefore to be admired.

Four corners of my world

The retreating sea has left in every indentation of the rocks a little pool, and in the pools we find starfish, jellyfish, sea anemones, and small green twists of seaweed. We poke the jellyfish with twigs to make them squirt. We watch a snail moving almost imperceptibly across the wet sand. We take off our shoes and socks and the cold waves run over our ankles, then we continue along the beach to where a brown river, still full from the rainy season, joins the sea. It rushes down in veins across the sand. This is a place for racing sticks and betting trillions of dollars on the outcome. It is a place empty of all save ourselves and gulls and sandpipers.

Later we return to the rocks where we perch, watching the sun go down and the tide come in, a ceremony we know by heart. The sky fills with turquoise, rose, gold, then the sun sinks, sucked in by the sea. When the sea surrounds the rocks we wade to shore. On the way home our friend tells us her mother is an invalid. We don't know the meaning of the word invalid and are afraid to ask in case it should mean two-headed. At the bottom of the cliff we say good-bye, for there is no twilight; after the explosion of the setting sun an explosion of stars. We climb the path to Bamboo-land where we sit before the fire and toast salt-caked toes. In California we have meals with our mother, even dinner. Tonight, as a separate course, artichokes: leaves to be plucked, dipped in melted butter, nibbled at, then stacked in symmetrical heaps until at last the heart is revealed, a delicacy to equate with nightingales' tongues or the heart of a virgin.

Mr. Hesketh, our freckled friend's father, asks us to Sunday lunch. The Spanish moss that hangs from the live-oak trees that crowd his house turns to the grey hair of witches as we approach. An air of mourning seeps from the windows. Our lively friend is sober and quiet. Mr. Hesketh and our mother carry the awkward burden of conversation. During lunch I sense grey tears oozing from the floor, the ceiling, the walls. I taste grey tears in my food. I do not know who is weeping or why.

Later, when our friend takes us to inspect a flock of goats, the gloom temporarily lifts. But on our return to the verandah we learn from Mr. Hesketh that our mother is with the invalid and that we are to join her. We can't very well say 'No, thank you.'

At first I see nothing but the greenish dark, then gradually a face emerges from the pillows and a weak, plaintive voice asks us how we do. She tells us she only eats a leaf of lettuce a day, and we believe her for she is thin as the dead. The windows are closed, and the shutters, against the sun. The air smells old and sour.

Later we learn from our mother that she is sick because she thinks she's sick. And the grey tears come, not from one but from three – father, mother, and child.

We never return to the brown house in the foothills, though our mother occasionally visits the invalid and our friend still comes to play with us on the beach and Mr. Hesketh brings goats' milk – so much better than cows', he says, though we know it is not our health that concerns him but the hope of glimpsing our beautiful mother.

My mother was reserved and quiet but she enjoyed her opposites. She found one in Mrs. Sykes who lived across the railroad track and round the corner from Bambooland. She was cockney and married to an old and affluent Englishman – a gentleman. Mrs. Sykes said so.

We thought him a princely character and lavish with his wealth, for sometimes when we passed him on the road he gave us a dime, but Mrs. Sykes said no, he was mean as they come. 'I was a nurse,' she went on, 'and he wanted someone to take care of him. And I wanted a bit of money. Well, when we sailed for America we walked up different gangplanks – he to first class, me to third. Our 'oneymoon,' she ended, laughing till the tears ran down her face.

Mrs. Sykes was a strategist. She plotted and worked for peace in the home, for her husband was a man of uninhibited temper.

Four corners of my world

One day catastrophe struck. Prohibition still ruled the land and a man's cellar and his dearest treasure were synonymous.

'Robbers,' said Mrs. Sykes to my mother. 'They took all the bottles and left the taps of the kegs turned on. Cellar's flooded with whisky. Can't tell Mr. Sykes. He'd have a stroke.' So she bided her time.

A week later a friend was run over by a train a few hundred yards from their house. 'It just came to me, Mary,' she said to Mother later, 'that if I told him about poor Mildred and the whisky at the same time I'd be saving him and me from a tantrum.' It worked. Being a gentleman, he could only mourn for his friend.

My mother had been brought up on family prayers and church on Sunday, but she lost her faith and our religious instruction had been vague and our church-going erratic. So we were surprised, though not dismayed, when we became regular attendants at Christ-Church-by-the-Sea. Our mother knew the rector and believed him to be an intelligent and spiritual man. He had lost a leg, above the knee, and I learned that he suffered great pain in the non-existent limb. This positive pain in a no-leg seemed to me a kind of devil's magic, and for all his spirituality I fancied he had committed some crime in his youth for which he was paying with a supernatural agony.

Halfway through church the children of the congregation left for Sunday school. Sunday school I couldn't miss. There was something from Sunday school I wanted – a pin, blue and gold and shaped like a shield, the reward for attendance on twelve successive Sundays. We weren't allowed to wear jewellery, but no-one could stop me from wearing a Sunday-school pin, and I lusted for it as misers lust for gold. I can't remember whether I earned it or not. All I remember is desire.

On Easter Sunday the church was filled with lilies and resurrection. Door and windows were open to the sun and sea-drenched air. God was a gentle spirit in a golden world. I wore a new dotted Swiss dress and felt myself akin to angels. But Easter meant going back to Toronto, leaving Bambooland and the beach and the mountains, Yee and the lizards and school. It meant another governess and lessons in the billiard-room at Craigleigh.

Much of the time my sister and I did not go to school at all, and when we did it was usually to an extraordinary one such as the Ojai Valley School in California, thirty miles distant from Santa Barbara. My mother first learned of its existence from an article in the *Atlantic Monthly* by its founder and head, Mr. Yeomans.

Mr. Yeomans had made a comfortable fortune in business, and on retiring had invested a part of it in Utopia. He had read Dewey. He believed in the natural goodness of man. He also believed that in an environment of his making the natural goodness of children would prove self-evident. Though he came from the East and considered the Atlantic Ocean a superior water to the Pacific, he chose a Californian valley for his experiment. Climate decided him.

Sun was a necessary component of the ideal life. This was to be our first boarding-school, indeed our first full year at any school. The prospectus promised something out of the ordinary: boys as well as girls, and in class only such subjects as Mr. Yeomans believed enlightening. Teachers, to qualify, must be married, and fruitful as well, else how should they divine the multiple needs of children?

We believed we were going to Paradise, yet the signposts, though so obviously of gold, were different from those at home, and we shivered as certain priests do when they lie dying.

Up, up a narrow, tortuous mountain road, then down into a valley lined with orange groves and lemon. In the distance, on our left, is the school, and before we know it Mr. Yeomans is shaking our mother by the hand. He looks like a seaman and his gait has a roll to it – a shaggy man with a gruff, compassionate voice. I am immediately afraid for him, sensing that he is a dreamer and that I shall be one of his nightmares. I'm a troublemaker unless I have a vast share of everyone's attention. The family have adjusted to my demands, but this is not home.

Next we meet Mr. and Mrs. Lejeune who stand second in command to Mr. Yeomans. Mr. Lejeune resembles Auden or someone of that ilk. His teeth are too big or he has too many of them. He is English and his grey flannel trousers are short and the press gone out of them. Yet somehow all this adds up to a seemly whole, and we soon learn that he is both gentle and just, a man of honour and delicate sensibilities. His wife is pretty and crisp and so British that she will always be a stranger outside an English shire. The Lejeunes have, as diploma, two children, Diana and Michael.

Mr. and Mrs. Brown and Mr. and Mrs. Bell are New Englanders. Mr. and Mrs. Brown have two-year-old Joan as proof of eligibility, and Mr. and Mrs. Bell are only three months wed so there is unquestionably hope.

Our mother leaves and we unpack. Every child has a room of its own. Friendly Amazons, big sun-burned girls, stand around and question us and give advice. They tell us the nights are still mild, that they are all sleeping on the porch where, with their help, we immediately move our beds.

The Amazons are more sophisticated yet more childlike than ourselves. They are vigorous outdoor creatures, and I watch enviously while one bounces a ball with a hundred variations and a rhyme for each and another turns cartwheels up and down the length of the porch. How can I distinguish myself in the face of such talents?

When I learn the rising bell rings at six-thirty I recognize the serpent in paradise.

Mr. Lejeune, Mr. Brown, and Mr. Bell teach, their wives mother (affection very important). But a time comes when morning sickness sends one or all rushing from the breakfast-table and they soon relinquish communal motherhood for more intimate private enterprise. Their husbands are forced to take over. To them falls the duty of seeing that we go to bed on time, that our teeth are brushed, that we take the requisite number of baths. For them the duty of the good-night kiss (affection more important than ever).

All the girls are in love with Mr. Lejeune or Mr. Brown. Mr. Bell arouses no erotic emotions among his pupils. But our passions do not always stand them in good stead. In the bathroom, though there is no lock on the door, we are safe as in a fortress. If Mr. Brown raps and orders us out we answer roguishly that we prefer to stay where we are, that he can't come in because we are naked. We also compare notes on the good-night kisses, on how long we have been able to keep the beloved sitting on the bed.

Our love for the teachers prevents any very heavy affairs between the boys and girls, the oldest of whom are not more than fifteen, for Mr. Yeomans's disregard of university requirements has decided him to set an age limit. Fifteen is a paltry thing as compared with twenty-seven. Mr. Brown is twenty-seven and I recognize nothing less.

As the months pass the swelling bellies of the wives give a quite exceptional air of fecundity to our place of learning, and though in theory Mr. Yeomans is all for nature, in actual fact he is embarrassed by so much burgeoning womanhood. Sex alarms him. Sex seems always about to shatter his Utopia.

Mrs. Yeomans is from Boston and affects the dowdy clothes of her townswomen. She has no official position in the school but her nose is everywhere. Virtue she may have but no charm. We believe her unworthy of her mate, who is loved and respected even by the unregenerate.

The Shop, a long low building with a fire-place at one end and smelling sweetly of wood shavings, is Mr. Yeomans's domain. Here beautiful things are made: bows and arrows and ships and covered wagons. To work a part of each day with one's hands is the core of Mr. Yeomans's creed, the highroad to grace and happiness. Clumsy hands combined with indifference soon disqualified me from the ranks of the blessed. But something else happens in the shop that is illuminating even to inept carpenters. Here Mr. Yeomans reads *Hamlet* in his deep, gruff voice. This big bear of a man was the best Ophelia I have ever heard.

Folk dance and folk song are favoured subjects. Miss Spinner, who shame to say is unwed and likely to remain so, supervises the dance. The boys despise the sport and the girls incline to giggles, so Ye Olde Merrie England is merry enough in its way but does not exactly correspond to Mr. Yeomans's concept of the light fantastic.

Mr. Bell leads the singing – folk songs, sea shanties, and Bach chorales. He has a pink face and a pink scalp that shows through pale skimpy hair, pale blue eyes and rimless glasses, and no idea in the world how to manage children. As I cannot sing in tune, I make a shambles of his class. Later, when I reform, the music becomes a part of me and I love it almost as much as those who can sing.

With my clumsy hands and an uncertain voice I am singularly ill-equipped for progressive education. I find the conventional classroom subjects more to my taste, though here too I am sufficiently obstreperous to be dismissed from all save those of Mr. Brown. This suits me very well until Mr. Yeomans calls me into the Shop and with a grave face tells me he is sending me home. I have become his nightmare, proving the exception to his belief in the natural goodness of children. Remorse. Also fear of the shock it will inflict on my mother. I tell him she is away, that he can't send me to a house empty except for a Chinese cook. I vow I will become one of the angels of his paradise. Mr. Yeomans relents, and though I never become a first-class angel, I enter rooms by way of doors instead of windows and I try to be a good carpenter. I return to the classrooms from which I had been banished.

My first lesson from Mr. Lejeune is a demonstration, with bits of wire and electricity, of why the bell rings when you press the button. It is apparently a not-too-difficult problem, as everyone else comprehends the facts. After class is dismissed Mr. Lejeune keeps me in for a private bell-ringing lesson. Patiently he demonstrates, patiently he repeats something about positives and negatives, patiently I listen. To no avail. For three days he persists and then, worn out by what he believes to be my stubbornness, he gives up, leaving me to pick my way through life innocent of why the bell rings when you push the button.

From Mr. and Mrs. Brown I learn, though not in the classroom, of Freud and dreams, and a great deal of minutiae about sex. They colour my primitive knowledge of the Facts of Life with pictures of sperm wiggle-waggling their way through tunnels and tubes to the placid ovum. Not altogether unlike why the bell rings when you press the button but at the time I do not observe the connection.

My newly acquired Freudian jargon gives me a fine sense of my own sophistication, and I grieve, when I try it on my mother, at its cold reception.

But Freud and folk dancing, carpentry and sex and electricity, are a far cry from a governess, and the Kings of England in the billiard-room at Craigleigh.

NOTES

Notes on manuscript sources and texts

AFTER READING KAFKA (p. 25). The second to last line on p. 26 reads 'Do flora deera fawn breathe on?' as printed in *Counterpoint to Sleep*, an obvious error. I have risked changing it to 'Do flora, deer and fawn breathe on?'

THE GREAT WINDS (p. 31). L. 13 reads 'A lung, our pledge to plunge from stilla water' in *Counterpoint to Sleep*. After some hesitation I have printed this here as 'A lung, our pledge to plunge from a still water'.

DIRGE (p. 73). This poem appears in an early draft of *The Hangman* volume under the title 'Nursery Rhyme' and with two stanzas later deleted. They follow stanza four and are as follows:

> Who'll bear the pall?
> We, said the children,
> Heirs to their burden,
> We bear the pall.

> Who'll dig the grave?
> I said the lawyer,
> I know the procedure,
> I'll dig the grave.

LETTER TO MY CHILDREN (p. 94). Early drafts of *The Hangman* contain the whole poem, but only the first three stanzas appear in the printed volume. In one manuscript the author pencilled in the heading P.S., and I have felt justified in placing the fine major portion of the poem at the head of the uncollected pieces under the title 'Letter to My Children: Postscript' (p. 127).

NATURE BE DAMNED (p. 109). First published in *Tamarack Review*, No. 5, Autumn 1957. When this poem was reprinted in *The Oxford Book of Canadian Verse* (1960) Anne Wilkinson added a new section between parts III and IV:

> I took my watch beside the rose;
> I saw the worm move in;
> And by the tail I yanked him out
> And stamped him dead, for who would choose
> To leave alive a sin.

> The pale rose died of grief. My heel
> Had killed its darling foe,
> Worm that cuddles in the heart
> To ravish it. If worm not tell
> How should rose its fairness know?

Notes

The *Oxford Book* has a later, but I think inferior, last line of section 1: 'For none may live if all do love'.

VARIATIONS ON A THEME (p. 112) first published in *Tamarack Review* No. 5, Autumn 1957.

A CAUTIONARY TALE (p. 115). In *Oxford Book of Canadian Verse*, 1960.

FALCONRY (p. 117). In *Oxford Book of Canadian Verse*, 1960.

NOTES ON ROBERT BURTON'S 'THE ANATOMY OF MELANCHOLY' (p. 119). First published in *Tamarack Review*, No. 18, Winter 1961.

BALLAD (p. 136). In one version of this poem the word 'guilty' in the last line is crossed out in pencil and the word 'practised' substituted.

I WAS WITCH, OR SKILLED MAGICIAN (p. 143). This is an earlier version of *Nature be damned*, 111.

FISHWIFE (p. 165). The last three lines of this poem are given as in the latest version – a manuscript given to the editor. In most other typescripts these lines read:

> *With jumping wand you charm alive*
> *A woman's thighs, that we may love*
> *Without impediment.*

A SORROW OF STONES 1. SONG (p. 170). A shorter version of this poem appears in some of the manuscripts.

> *In this graveyard, hedged, they lie*
> *A lady and her gardener.*
> *Across the hedge their garden grows*
> *Cabbage coarse, corn on high*
> *And pretty pods all in a row.*
>
> *Only flowers wilt and die*
> *Of love for lost green thumbs.*
> *More than sun and rain they seek.*
> *Not by rain and sun alone.*
> *In the rosebed, tree of stone.*

The first two lines in one version are as follows:

> *In this graveyard, hedged, they lie,*
> *My mother and her gardener –*

with the word 'dumb' pencilled in over 'hedged'.